Table of Contents

Part 1
Grammar, Usage, and Mechanics

Unit 1 The Sentence
1 Kinds of Sentences	1
▶ Revising Strategies: Sentence Fluency Writing Good Sentences	3
2 Complete Subjects and Complete Predicates	5
3 Simple Subjects and Simple Predicates	7
▶ Revising Strategies: Sentence Fluency Forming Compound Subjects and Compound Predicates	9
4 Finding the Subject	11
5 Conjunctions	13
6 Fragments and Run-ons	15
▶ Revising Strategies: Sentence Fluency Forming Compound Sentences and Complex Sentences	17

Unit 2 Nouns
1 Kinds of Nouns	19
2 Collective and Compound Nouns	21
3 Singular and Plural Nouns	23
▶ Revising Strategies: Sentence Fluency Writing with Nouns	25
4 Possessive Nouns	27
▶ Revising Strategies: Sentence Fluency Writing with Possessive Nouns	29
▶ Revising Strategies: Vocabulary Exact Nouns	31

Unit 3 Verbs
1 Kinds of Verbs	32
2 Verb Phrases	34
3 Simple Verb Tenses	36
4 *be, have,* and *do*	38
5 Perfect Tenses	40
6 Irregular Verbs	42
7 More Irregular Verbs	44
8 Progressive Forms	46
▶ Revising Strategies: Sentence Fluency Writing with Verbs	48
9 Transitive and Intransitive Verbs	50
10 Direct and Indirect Objects	52
11 Predicate Nouns and Predicate Adjectives	54
12 Active and Passive Voices	56
▶ Revising Strategies: Sentence Fluency Writing with Verbs	58
13 Subject-Verb Agreement	60
14 Inverted and Interrupted Order	62
15 *rise, raise; lie, lay; sit, set*	64
16 *bring, take; let, leave; lend, loan*	66
▶ Revising Strategies: Vocabulary Choosing Different Verbs	68

Unit 4 Modifiers
1 Adjectives	69
▶ Revising Strategies: Sentence Fluency Writing with Adjectives	71
2 Comparing with Adjectives	73
3 Adverbs	75
▶ Revising Strategies: Sentence Fluency Writing with Adverbs	77
4 Comparing with Adverbs	79
5 Negatives	81
6 Adjective or Adverb?	83
▶ Revising Strategies: Vocabulary Choosing Different Adjectives and Adverbs	85

Unit 5 Capitalization and Punctuation
1 Correct Sentences	86
2 Proper Nouns and Proper Adjectives	88
3 Interjections	90
4 Uses for Commas	92
▶ Revising Strategies: Sentence Fluency Writing Sentences with Commas	94
5 More Uses for Commas	96
6 Dates, Addresses, and Letters	98
7 Direct Quotations	100
8 Titles	102
9 Semicolons and Colons	104
▶ Revising Strategies: Sentence Fluency Writing Sentences with Semicolons and Colons	106
10 Abbreviations	108
11 Apostrophes	110
12 Hyphens, Dashes, and Parentheses	112

Unit 6 Pronouns
1 Pronouns and Antecedents	114
▶ Revising Strategies: Sentence Fluency Writing Clearly with Pronouns	116
2 Personal Pronouns	118
3 Subject and Object Pronouns	120
4 Pronouns in Compound Subjects and Objects	122
5 Possessive Pronouns	124
6 Interrogative Pronouns	126
7 Demonstrative Pronouns	128
8 Indefinite Pronouns	130
9 Reflexive and Intensive Pronouns	132
▶ Revising Strategies: Vocabulary Homophones	134

Unit 7 Prepositional Phrases

1 Prepositional Phrases	135
2 Pronouns After Prepositions	137
3 Adjective Phrases	139
4 Adverb Phrases	141
5 Placing Phrases Correctly	143
▶ Revising Strategies: Sentence Fluency Writing with Prepositional Phrases	145
6 Choosing Correct Prepositions	147
▶ Revising Strategies: Vocabulary Idioms	149

Unit 8 Complex Sentences

1 Clauses	150
2 Compound and Complex Sentences	152
▶ Revising Strategies: Sentence Fluency Forming Complex and Compound-Complex Sentences	154

Part 2
Writing, Listening, Speaking, and Viewing

Section 1 Expressing and Influencing

Getting Started: Opinion Paragraphs Supporting Sentences	156

Unit 9 Writing to Express an Opinion

Supporting Your Opinion	157
Elaborating Your Reasons	158
Organizing Your Reasons	159
Writing with Voice	160
Introductions and Conclusions	161
Revising an Opinion Essay	162
The Writing Process: Revising Strategies Sentence Fluency	163

Unit 10 Writing to Persuade

Supporting Your Goal	164
Evaluating Your Reasons	165
Using Persuasive Strategies	166
Organizing Your Argument	167
Introductions and Conclusions	168
Writing with Voice	169
Revising a Persuasive Essay	170
The Writing Process: Revising Strategies Elaborating: Details	171

Section 2 Explaining and Informing

Getting Started: Expository Paragraphs Supporting Sentences	172

Unit 11 Writing to Compare and Contrast

Organizing Your Essay	173
Introductions and Conclusions	174
Topic Sentences	175
Revising a Compare-Contrast Essay	176
The Writing Process: Revising Strategies Elaborating: Word Choice	177

Unit 12 Writing a Research Report

Finding the Best Information	178
Organizing Your Report	179
Writing from an Outline	180
Introductions and Conclusions	181
Revising a Research Report	182
The Writing Process: Revising Strategies Elaborating: High-Interest Details	183

Section 3 Narrating and Entertaining

Getting Started: Narrative Paragraphs Supporting Sentences	184

Unit 13 Writing a Personal Narrative

Organizing Your Narrative	185
Good Beginnings	186
Writing with Voice	187
Good Endings	188
Revising a Personal Narrative	189
The Writing Process: Revising Strategies Elaborating: Word Choice	190

Unit 14 Writing a Story

Developing Plot	191
Dialogue	192
Narrating Your Story	193
Revising a Story	194
The Writing Process: Revising Strategies Sentence Fluency	195

Grammar/Mechanics

Name _____

1 Kinds of Sentences

Declarative sentence	I am glad to see my friends in school.
Interrogative sentence	What did you do all summer?
Imperative sentence	Don't leave without me.
Exclamatory sentence	What a confusing day this is!

Write each sentence correctly. Label each one *D* for declarative, *INT* for interrogative, *IM* for imperative, or *E* for exclamatory.

1. There are lots of clubs at our school

2. Are you singing in the chorus this year

3. Do you know anyone in the band

4. Jessica is trying out for the field hockey team

5. Andy wants to be on the school newspaper

6. Do you think you'll make the track team this year

7. Sign up for the camera club

8. Please wait for me after school

9. What a great time we'll have at football games

10. How exciting this year will be

(continued)

Grade 7: Unit 1 The Sentence (Use with pupil book pages 32–34.)
Skill: Students will identify and will punctuate the four kinds of sentences.

UNIT 1 THE SENTENCE

WORKBOOK PLUS 1

Grammar/Mechanics

Name _____

1 Kinds of Sentences (continued from page 1)

Challenge

Suppose that something funny has happened to you on your first day in a new school. When you get home, a friend calls you on the phone. Write your conversation. Use the kinds of sentences named in parentheses.

Your friend says: (interrogative) _____
_____

You say: (declarative) _____
_____

Your friend says: (exclamatory) _____
_____

You say: (imperative) _____
_____

Write the last two lines of your phone conversation. Choose any of the four kinds of sentences.

Your friend says: _____
_____

You say: _____
_____
_____

Writing Application: Sentences —

Suppose that you are the captain of a school athletic team. Your coach left you in charge of yesterday's practice session. Write at least eight sentences, describing how you ran the session and how your teammates reacted. Include a declarative, an interrogative, an imperative, and an exclamatory sentence.

2 WORKBOOK PLUS

Grade 7: Unit 1 The Sentence (Use with pupil book pages 32–34.)
Skill: Students will identify and will write the four kinds of sentences.

Writing Good Sentences

Same sentence types	The Drumbubbles are coming to town. They are the newest rock group to play in this area. You can get tickets to their concert today. It will be a unique experience.
Varied sentence types	Did you know the Drumbubbles are coming to town? They are the newest rock group to play in this area. Get your tickets to their concert today. What a unique experience it will be!

Varying Sentence Types 1–4. Rewrite the description. Vary the type of four of the sentences.

Revising

Dilly and the Drumbubbles were holding a concert on Saturday. Shea had every one of their CDs. They were his favorite music group. He had $6.50 and needed $18.50 more. He did not know what he could do to earn the money he needed. His dad said that if he worked around the house he could earn the money.

Shea and his dad drew up a list of chores that were to be done within a week. Shea did not know if he could finish them in time. Over the next few days he washed windows, vacuumed rugs, and even painted the porch. There were only three more days to the concert. Shea finally completed his chores and bought a ticket. On the night before the concert, Shea heard the bad news. Dilly had a sore throat and the concert was canceled.

_____
_____
_____
_____
_____
_____
_____
_____

(continued)

Revising Strategies: Sentence Fluency

Name _____

Writing Good Sentences (continued from page 3)

Stringy sentence	Today we are going on the Internet in computer class and the first place we will visit is our school's own Web site, which we designed ourselves last year, when we were in the sixth grade.
Shorter sentences	Today we are going on the Internet in computer class. The first place we will visit is our school's own Web site. We designed this site ourselves last year, when we were in the sixth grade.

Correcting Stringy Sentences 5–8. Revise the paragraph. Divide the four stringy sentences into shorter ones.

> **Revising**
>
> Parth was drenched because his brother, Abee, had gotten him good with the hose and Abee knew that Parth would try to even the score, but how and when would Parth strike? Abee did not let on, but he was getting more and more nervous with each passing day, and it was two weeks now and still Parth had done nothing. Abee had been on guard the whole time, and he could think of nothing else and found it hard to eat and sleep, but finally he could take it no longer so he confronted Parth. Parth listened with a broad smile on his face and then told his brother that his plan was to do nothing, and then he said that he knew that Abee would expect him to get even, and that having Abee wait and wonder what would happen and when was his entire plan.

5. _____

6. _____

7. _____

8. _____

Grammar

Name _____

2 Complete Subjects and Complete Predicates

Complete Subjects	Complete Predicates
A man in Massachusetts	improved four-wheeled roller skates in 1863.
They	were a big hit.
Earlier skates	had only two wheels.

Write each sentence. Draw a line between the complete subject and the complete predicate.

1. The Dutch have enjoyed roller skating since the 1700s.

2. Their skates with four wheels made the sport popular.

3. It is still a popular sport today.

4. The wheels of the first roller skates often were made of wood.

5. These wooden wheels broke very easily.

6. They were soon replaced by steel wheels.

7. Roller skating races became popular in the late 1800s.

8. The sport of ice skating is much older than roller skating.

9. Northern Europeans had their own kind of ice skates long ago.

10. They tied pieces of bone to their shoes.

(continued)

Grade 7: Unit 1   The Sentence   (Use with pupil book pages 37–39.)
Skill: Students will identify complete subjects and complete predicates.

WORKBOOK PLUS 5

Grammar

Name _____

2 Complete Subjects and Complete Predicates (continued from page 5)

Challenge

Underline the complete subject and circle the complete predicate of each sentence.

1. The ancient Egyptians played a game similar to bowling.
           9   1   12 7

2. Equipment for this game has been found in an ancient Egyptian tomb.
      2   11   6   2

3. Bowling was a popular sport in Europe by the 1400s.
       7   1   4

4. It was played with nine pins at that time.
     4   11

5. King Henry VIII had bowling alleys in his palace.
       8   3 12   8

6. Dutch settlers were the first to bring the game to America.
     6   14   10 5

7. They added an extra pin to the game.
     5   14   9

8. Washington Irving describes this game of ten pins in "Rip Van Winkle."
      13   10   13   3

To find out the title of this story, look at the circled complete predicates. Write the numbered letters from these predicates in the boxes with the same numbers.

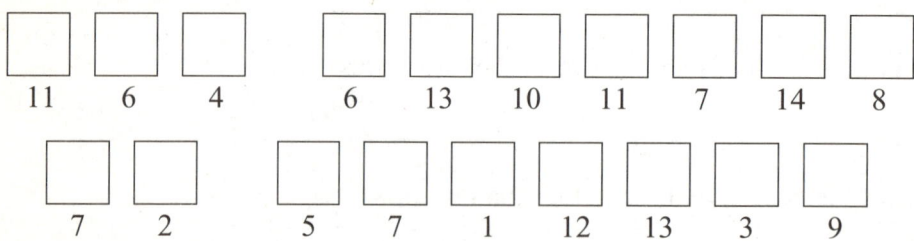

Writing Application: A Newspaper Article

Your class bowling team just won the seventh grade championship. Write an article about the final game of the championship. Draw a line between the complete subject and the complete predicate of each sentence.

3 Simple Subjects and Simple Predicates

Simple Subjects	Simple Predicates
Different **kinds** of shoes	**are worn** as fashions.
They	**have been worn** for protection too.
Thomas Saint of London	**invented** a machine to sew shoes.

For each sentence, underline the simple subject once and the simple predicate twice.

1. Shoes have been in existence for many centuries.
2. They protected feet from cold weather and rough surfaces.
3. People from cold climates wore fur boots.
4. Inhabitants of warm climates needed sandals for their feet.
5. Egyptians created sandals from plant fibers or leather.
6. Greeks wore this type of shoe too.
7. The ancient Chinese did not use these same materials.
8. They constructed their shoes from cloth.
9. American Indians made leather moccasins.
10. Simple tools were once used to make shoes.
11. Machines were first developed in the mid-1800s.
12. Jan Matzeliger was an American factory worker.
13. He invented an important machine in 1883.
14. This machine connected the upper part of the shoe to the sole.
15. His invention worked!
16. This new piece of machinery lowered the cost of production.
17. Most people have not heard of Matzeliger, however.
18. Machines manufacture most shoes today.

(continued)

Grade 7: Unit 1 The Sentence (Use with pupil book pages 40–42.)
Skill: Students will identify simple subjects and simple predicates.

Grammar

3 Simple Subjects and Simple Predicates (continued from page 7)

Challenge

The following letter from a pioneer woman is written in code. To solve the code, first underline the simple subject and the simple predicate of each sentence.

Dear Abigail,

(1) The baby rests quietly in the cradle. (2) I notice the beautiful sunset outside. (3) George has earned some extra money in town. (4) The land on our farm produces all of our food. (5) I am making our clothes for the winter. (6) Isabel Newley does not arrive until Thursday of next week. (7) Our neighbors grow the biggest tomatoes in the county. (8) Edith remembers your last visit fondly.

Your friend,

Betsy

Now write the first letter of each underlined simple subject and simple predicate. Write them in order in the blanks below.

___ ___ ___ ___ ___ ___ ___ ___ ___ ___ ___ ___ ___ ___ ___
___ ___ ___ ___ ___!

Writing Application: Sentence

Write at least five sentences, describing an invention that would make your life easier. Tell what the machine does and what it looks like. Underline the simple subject and circle the simple predicate of each sentence.

Revising Strategies: Sentence Fluency

Name _____

Forming Compound Subjects and Compound Predicates

Simple sentences	A top-quality camera helps a photographer take inspiring photos. An eye for detail helps a photographer take inspiring photographs.
Combined sentence	A top-quality camera **and** an eye for detail **help** a photographer take inspiring photographs.

Combining Sentences 1–5. Revise the paragraph. Combine each set of underlined sentences using compound subjects or compound predicates.

Revising

Jacob Riis was a great photographer. Lewis Hine was a great photographer. Photography was not their only achievement. Both men also wrote books. Both men also gave speeches. However, it was their photography that made them famous. Their pictures influenced many people. Their ideas influenced many people. Their words influenced many people. Riis and Hine were able to reach the public through their work. Photography fans can buy their books. Photography fans can see their pictures in a variety of museums. It is important to note that these artists had much in common. Their love of photography developed into a lasting and successful life's work. Their compassion for others developed into a lasting and successful life's work.

1. _____
_____
2. _____
3. _____
_____
4. _____
_____
5. _____

(continued)

Grade 7: Unit 1   The Sentence *(Use with pupil book pages 43–44.)*
Skill: Students will use compound subjects and compound predicates to combine sentences.

WORKBOOK PLUS 9

Forming Compound Subjects and Compound Predicates (continued from page 9)

General sentence	Architects work to earn their degrees.
Elaborated sentence	Architects study for six years and complete an architectural project to earn their degrees.

Elaborating Sentences 6–10. Revise the paragraph. Elaborate the underlined words or phrases. Replace each with a compound subject or compound predicate. Use details from the picture to help.

Revising

The buildings line the streets of the city. Each is interesting in its own way. People enter and leave them every day without taking notice. Different styles of buildings aligned on the same street make up a magnificent skyline. Outside the buildings people do things.

6. _____

7. _____

8. _____

9. _____

10. _____

4 Finding the Subject

Inverted Order	Imperatives
subject Next to my house is a **park**.	subject **(You)** Please ask her.
subject There is a **pool** in the park.	subject **(You)** Tell her to bring a towel.
subject Does **Theresa** want to go swimming?	subject **(You)** Don't be late.

Write the simple subject of each sentence.

1. How can I get to the park from here? _____
2. Here are the exact directions. _____
3. Do you see that traffic light next to the gas station? _____
4. Turn right there. _____
5. On the next corner is a blue house. _____
6. Is it the only blue house on the street? _____
7. Make a left there. _____
8. Should I write the directions on a sheet of paper? _____
9. Here is a pen. _____
10. Please write them carefully. _____
11. Continue on this street for six blocks. _____
12. There will be a hospital on your right. _____
13. Cross the next intersection. _____
14. On the other side of the street is Gerald Road. _____
15. Walk past the bank on the next corner. _____
16. Around the corner is Sandalwood Park. _____
17. Is there a pool in the park? _____
18. There are tennis courts too. _____

(continued)

Grade 7: Unit 1   The Sentence   (Use with pupil book pages 45–47.)
Skill: Students will identify simple subjects in inverted and imperative sentences.

Grammar

4 Finding the Subject (continued from page 11)

Challenge

Below are the directions from Arnold's house to his friend Danielle's house. The directions are not in the correct order. Number them correctly. Use the map at the bottom to help you.

SIMPLE SUBJECTS

_____ There is Danielle's house behind the playground.   _____

_____ Turn left at that sign.   _____

_____ Just past the tree is a playground.   _____

_____ Walk down Weston Street to Nelson Avenue.   _____

_____ Walk two blocks to Eliot Street.   _____

_____ There is a stop sign on that corner.   _____

_____ Do you see the oak tree on that corner?   _____

_____ Make a right at the oak.   _____

Now write the simple subject of each sentence above.

Writing Application: Directions — DESCRIBING

Suppose that a friend is asking you for directions from school to your home. Write a conversation in which your friend asks questions and you answer them with the correct directions. Include at least two declarative sentences in inverted order, two interrogative sentences, and two imperative sentences.

Grammar/Usage

5 Conjunctions

Coordinating Conjunctions	Correlative Conjunctions
and but or	both . . . and either . . . or whether . . . or neither . . . nor
Is cantaloupe, watermelon, **or** honeydew your favorite melon? **Both** California **and** Georgia supply melons for many states.	

A Write the coordinating conjunction or correlative conjunctions that best complete each sentence.

1. Oranges _____ lemons are citrus fruits.

2. Citrus fruits are usually _____ orange _____ yellow.

3. These fruits contain _____ vitamins _____ minerals.

4. _____ you eat them _____ drink the juice, you get vitamin C.

5. You can buy orange juice _____ squeeze your own.

6. Oranges can be hard to peel, _____ tangerines peel easily.

7. _____ lemons _____ limes are high in calories.

B 8–12. This recipe has five incorrect conjunctions. Use proofreading marks to correct the recipe.

Example: It is fun to make your own fruit punch. The directions below provide a quick or̂ easy recipe. *(and inserted above)*

Proofreading Marks	
¶	Indent
∧	Add
⌒	Delete
≡	Capital letter
/	Small letter
⌄⌄ ⌄⌄	Add quotes
∧	Add comma
⊙	Add period
∽	Transpose

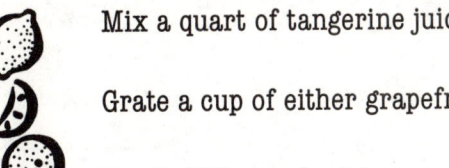

Tangerine Lime Punch

Mix a quart of tangerine juice but a liter of soda water.

Grate a cup of either grapefruit peel and orange peel.

Use half the peel mixture now or save the rest for another recipe.

Add half a cup of lime juice, or don't use lemon juice because it's sour.

Chill the punch for 1 and 2 hours.

(continued)

Grade 7: Unit 1 The Sentence *(Use with pupil book pages 48–50.)*
Skill: Students will use coordinating and correlative conjunctions.

Grammar/Usage

Name _____

5 Conjunctions (continued from page 13)

Challenge

Make up a riddle about a kind of food. Fill in the blanks, using the clues in parentheses. Write a conjunction in each box.

It is _____ ☐ tastes _____ . You
     (color or shape)   (how?)

can _____ ☐ _____ it.
     (cook how?)   (cook how?)

Both _____ ☐ _____ are used to flavor
     (name of food)   (name of food)

this food. _____ ☐ _____ are good
          (name of food)   (name of food)

things to eat with it. I like it best _____ , ☐ some
                        (fixed how?)

people prefer it _____ . I usually eat it for _____ ,
         (fixed how?)   (which meal?)

☐ sometimes I eat it _____ . This food is not
                 (when?)

_____ ☐ _____ .
 (name of food)   (name of food)

Ask your classmates to read your riddle and guess what food you've described.

Writing Application: A Letter — *INSTRUCTING*

Imagine that you are the owner of a food store. Write a letter to one of your suppliers, telling what food items you will need. Use at least two pairs of correlative conjunctions and three coordinating conjunctions.

Usage/Mechanics

Name _____

6 Fragments and Run-ons

Fragment	Elected Margaret Chase Smith to Congress.
Sentence	The people elected Margaret Chase Smith to Congress.
Run-on	Smith became a senator in 1948, she was re-elected three times.
Compound sentence	Smith became a senator in 1948, and she was re-elected three times.
Separate sentences	Smith became a senator in 1948. She was re-elected three times.

A 1–3. Rewrite the paragraph, correcting all the fragments and the run-ons.

    A woman was appointed to the United States Supreme Court in 1981, she is Judge Sandra Day O'Connor of Arizona. According to the U.S. Constitution. Justices are appointed by the President and approved by the Senate. The new justice has been a lawyer and a judge, she was also a state senator. Earned her law degree. At Stanford University.

_____
_____
_____
_____
_____
_____

B 4–6. This article has three errors with fragments. Use proofreading marks to correct the errors.

Example: Justice O'Connor earned her law degree⌐At Stanford University.

Proofreading Marks
- ¶ Indent
- ∧ Add
- ꝺ Delete
- ≡ Capital letter
- / Small letter
- ˇˇ Add quotes
- ∧, Add comma
- ⊙ Add period
- ∽ Transpose

Proofreading

    Ruth Bader Ginsburg was the second woman to be appointed to the U.S. Supreme Court. She faced many challenges. Before she was appointed to the Supreme Court. After she got her law degree. She practiced. And taught law.

(continued)

Grade 7: Unit 1 The Sentence *(Use with pupil book pages 51–54.)*
Skill: Students will write sentences that do not contain fragments or run-ons.

Usage/Mechanics

Name _____

6 Correcting Fragments and Run-ons (continued from page 15)

Challenge

A friend of yours is running for the Student Council. You have been asked to make a speech, explaining why this person should be elected. Below are your notes. Turn the notes into sentences by correcting any run-ons and fragments. Be sure to punctuate each sentence correctly.

Miguel cares about our class, he will listen to everyone's ideas.
Helps out at money-raising events, organizes class trips.
Because of willingness to work hard.
My friend's attitude toward other students.
My friend's talent.
Can work well with teachers and other adults.
Miguel always lends a hand, he'll help anyone in need.
Miguel debates well, he can easily persuade others.
Uses reason and good sense.
This friend listens, he makes fair decisions, he has great ideas.
Knows how to get things done, is confident, a good leader.

_____
_____
_____
_____
_____
_____
_____
_____
_____
_____

Writing Application: A Paragraph — EXPLAINING

Pretend that you have just attended an assembly where the candidates for student government gave their election speeches. Write about your favorite candidate. Tell what convinced you to vote for this person. Include compound sentences in your paragraph. Be sure that you have not written any fragments or run-ons.

Revising Strategies: Sentence Fluency

Name _____

Forming Compound Sentences and Complex Sentences

Simple sentences	Some trees provide shade. Others give us food.
Compound sentence	Some trees provide shade, **and** others give us food.

Combining Sentences: Compound Sentences 1–5. Combine each underlined pair of simple sentences into one compound sentence. Use the conjunction *and, but,* or *or* to join them.

> **Revising**
>
> <u>Cinnamon comes from tropical evergreens in Sri Lanka. Cork comes from cork oak trees in the Mediterranean.</u> Cinnamon and cork are actually the bark of these trees. <u>The bark of the cork oak is stripped every nine years. This process does not harm the tree.</u> There are many uses for these by-products of trees. <u>Cork can be made into floats. It can be used as insulation.</u> Other purposes exist as well. <u>Cinnamon is used in baking. It can be added as a flavor to drinks.</u>
> Keep in mind that trees are part of our natural resources. <u>Do you think we should cut them down indiscriminately? Do you think we should be more conservative?</u>

1. _____

2. _____

3. _____

4. _____

5. _____

(continued)

Grade 7: Unit 1 The Sentence *(Use with pupil book pages 55–56.)*
  Skill: Students will use a comma and a conjunction to combine simple sentences into a compound sentence.

WORKBOOK PLUS 17

Revising Strategies: Sentence Fluency

Name _____

Forming Compound Sentences and Complex Sentences *(continued from page 17)*

Simple sentences	We continued to harvest the crops. Our baskets were full.
Complex sentence	We continued to harvest the crops **until** our baskets were full.

Combining Sentences: Complex Sentences 6–10. Combine each underlined pair of simple sentences into one complex sentence. Use a subordinating conjunction such as *since*, *after*, or *because* to join them.

Revising

  Much of the conflict was fought on Southern soil. The Civil War devastated the cities in the South. The South suffered many other losses because of the war. Plantation owners still had land at the end of the war. They did not have labor. Sharecropping arose as a result. The plantation owners realized that help was needed to raise crops. They gave poor people a few acres of land and a cabin in exchange for a large share of the crops raised. Sharecroppers most often raised only one crop. The soil became depleted. Southern farmers realized the problem. They began using diversified agriculture.
  The economy of the South was also destroyed. The war depleted the wealth needed to support the army. The Civil War took its toll on every aspect of Southern living.

6. _____

7. _____

8. _____

9. _____

10. _____

Grade 7: Unit 1   The Sentence   *(Use with pupil book pages 55–56.)*
Skill: Students will combine two similar sentences into one complex sentence, using a subordinating conjunction.

Grammar

1 Kinds of Nouns

Concrete Nouns	Abstract Nouns	Common Nouns	Proper Nouns
mountain	justice	dentist	Dr. Magill
avenue	happiness	author	Mark Twain
Aunt Thelma	liberty	state	Hawaii
farmer	fairness	monument	Statue of Liberty

Write each noun. Label it *concrete* or *abstract* and then *common* or *proper*.

1. The first watch for the wrist was introduced in Switzerland.

2. Jacquet-Droz helped develop the successful idea.

3. Women wore these new and expensive items.

4. The most famous example belonged to Empress Josephine.

5. Parisian jewelers improved upon the design.

6. Eventually the invention became popular for men too.

7. The German Admiralty ordered many watches.

8. In World War I, the timepieces were worn frequently.

9. Modern clocks have fancy digital features.

(continued)

Grade 7: Unit 2 Nouns *(Use with pupil book pages 70–72.)*
Skill: Students will identify concrete, abstract, common, and proper nouns.

Grammar

1 Kinds of Nouns (continued from page 19)

Challenge

Suppose that you could be anything that you wanted to be! Would you choose to be a bird or a movie star? Write the one thing that you would be if you could select something from each category listed below. Write a concrete or an abstract noun to tell specifically what you would be. Then write a sentence explaining your selection.

1. An animal: _____

2. Another person: _____

3. A plant: _____

4. A machine: _____

5. A building: _____

6. A song: _____

7. An idea: _____

Now label each noun in your sentences *common* or *proper*.

Writing Application: A Paragraph

Suppose that you have just arrived in a strange land that has no clocks, watches, or calendars. Write a paragraph that describes your feelings about being in this land. Use concrete, abstract, common, and proper nouns.

Grade 7: Unit 2 Nouns (Use with pupil book pages 70–72.)
Skill: Students will use concrete, abstract, common, and proper nouns.

2 Collective and Compound Nouns

Collective Nouns	Compound Nouns
Congress	tennis shoe
fleet	son-in-law
committee	San Diego
herd	sunset

Write each sentence. Underline each collective noun once and each compound noun twice.

1. The world is made up of different groups.

2. The animal kingdom includes herds and packs.

3. A pride of lions hunts as a team on an African grassland.

4. A colony of fire ants builds its nest in a back yard in Texas.

5. High over the fields, a flock of Canada geese forms a giant V.

6. Off the Gulf Coast, a school of dolphins performs playful back flips.

7. Think of your family, your class, and your school as a whole.

8. The make-up of our society is a unique hodgepodge.

(continued)

Grammar

2 Collective and Compound Nouns (continued from page 21)

Challenge

You are a new member of a group called The Totally Left-handed. The club is holding a meeting to discuss some extremely important issues. The announcement below describes the agenda for this week's meeting. Fill in each blank with a collective or a compound noun.

The _____ for The Totally Left-handed meets today at noon. Members will draft a letter to _____. Our _____ wants to change the Constitution of the United States. We left-handers feel that this document overuses the word *rights*. Our master plan is to change half of the *rights* to *lefts*. The Bill of Rights would become the _____. Our _____ also wants the buttons on TV sets placed on the left.

To find the club room, turn left at the end of the _____. The society accepts all people. We even accept _____!

Now write five more sentences to describe this group. Include a collective or a compound noun in each sentence.

_____
_____
_____
_____
_____

Writing Application: A Job Application — INFORMING

Suppose that you are applying for a job. You are asked to list the groups that you belong to. Make the list. Then describe the purpose and activities of one of the clubs or organizations. Underline each collective noun. Circle each compound noun.

22 WORKBOOK PLUS

Grade 7: Unit 2 Nouns (Use with pupil book pages 73–75.)
Skill: Students will write collective and compound nouns.

3 Singular and Plural Nouns

Singular	cap	case	box	ditch	spy	tray	roof	life
Plural	cap**s**	case**s**	box**es**	ditch**es**	sp**ies**	tray**s**	roof**s**	li**ves**

Singular	waltz	piano	tomato	foot	son-in-law	news	deer
Plural	waltz**es**	piano**s**	tomato**es**	f**ee**t	son**s**-in-law	news	deer

Write the plural form of the noun in parentheses to complete each sentence.

1. One hundred has two _____ in it. **(zero)**
2. Many _____ sat in the tree. **(monkey)**
3. The _____ over the phone are annoying. **(buzz)**
4. How many _____ are there in six hundred sixty? **(six)**
5. Those _____ have to be mailed by midnight. **(entry)**
6. The _____ of the cattle sounded like thunder. **(hoof)**
7. Both _____ attended the party. **(mother-in-law)**
8. All my _____ must be mended. **(pants)**
9. The team has suffered a number of _____. **(loss)**
10. The _____ met for an hour. **(major general)**
11. Where did you buy those beautiful _____? **(candlestick)**
12. Two of my _____ must be filled. **(tooth)**
13. The weathered houses had sagging _____. **(roof)**
14. Would you add some _____ to the salad? **(tomato)**
15. Can you tell me the _____ of the day? **(news)**
16. Please help me carry these _____ to the barn. **(stone)**
17. Grandfather made two _____ this morning. **(lunch)**
18. How many _____ are in the show? **(cocker spaniel)**

(continued)

Grade 7: Unit 2 Nouns (Use with pupil book pages 76–78.)
Skill: Students will write the plural forms of nouns.

Grammar

3 Singular and Plural Nouns (continued from page 23)

Challenge

Suppose that you edit scripts for a movie company. Below is part of a script from your worst writer. Cross out any incorrect plural nouns. Then write the correct plurals above them.

Ron Rich: Timeses are hard, Vera. I'm working like ten donkies.

Vera Rich: Yes, brother, it's work just to keep rooves over our heades.

Ron: Why, today I bought only thirty ant farmes and sold fifty ranchs.

Vera: That's OK. I sold only three diamond mineses and bought a couple of saddle companys.

Ron: My brother-in-laws are a bigger problem. They're after my bank accounties.

Vera: Don't they know that all your moneys is invested in cattles?

Ron: No, they don't. Those relativeses just keep asking about my savinges.

Vera: Don't worry about those people. They're just small potatos, Ron.

Ron: It's not the dollares. It's a question of beliefes.

Mother Rich: What are you childrenes complaining about? Are you putting your foots in your mouthes again? Stop complaining and polish my jeweles.

Ron and Vera: I guess that chores come before economics in the Rich household!

Writing Application: A Diary Entry — NARRATING

Suppose that you toured an animal preserve in Africa. Your sunglasses made you see everything double. Write a diary entry, describing what you saw. Use at least one plural noun in each sentence.

Revising Strategies: Sentence Fluency

Writing with Nouns

Simple sentences	Herculaneum was destroyed in A.D. 79. Herculaneum was a Roman resort town.
Combined sentence	Herculaneum, **a Roman resort town,** was destroyed in A.D. 79.

Combining and Elaborating Sentences: Appositives 1–5. Revise the paragraph. Use appositives to combine each pair of underlined sentences.

> **Revising**
>
> Centuries ago a volcano erupted above a Roman resort town. <u>The volcano was Mount Vesuvius.</u> The destruction was immense. <u>Vesuvius spewed a glowing avalanche. The avalanche was a cloud of hot ash and gases.</u> This disaster occurred in Herculaneum. <u>Herculaneum was buried in minutes. It was a beautiful city by the sea.</u> We are now learning what happened to this ancient city. <u>Archaeologists are uncovering Herculaneum. These archaeologists are discoverers of ancient cities.</u> Discoveries help uncover many ancient mysteries. <u>Two sciences increase our knowledge of ancient life. The sciences are archaeology and anthropology.</u>

1. _____
2. _____
3. _____
4. _____
5. _____

(continued)

Grade 7: Unit 2 Nouns *(Use with pupil book pages 79–80.)*
Skill: Students will use appositives to combine sentences.

WORKBOOK PLUS 25

Revising Strategies: Sentence Fluency

Writing with Nouns (continued from page 25)

Simple sentence	My pet is sleeping on the windowsill.
Elaborated sentence	My pet, **a very independent kitten**, is sleeping on the windowsill.

Combining Sentences and Elaborating Sentences: Appositives 6–10. Revise the paragraph. Add appositives to elaborate each underlined noun. Use details from your own experience and your imagination.

Revising

Mike and Max were hardly ever apart. If Max could go to school with Mike, he would. However, the sign on the fence read "No Dogs Allowed." Max was certainly smart enough to attend <u>school</u>. He loved to be loved and was easily trained. Max did, in fact, get to go to school once. <u>Mike</u> had spent a week teaching Max to count. When Mike held up one finger, Max would bark and tap his foot once. <u>The dog</u> could count in this way up to five. Mike's <u>classmates</u> started to shout when Mike brought Max out on stage at a school assembly. Not only did Max count to five, but he solved addition problems to the sums of five. Even <u>the principal</u> stood up and clapped at the end of the show.

Grammar/Mechanics

Name _____

4 Possessive Nouns

Singular Possessive Nouns	Plural Possessive Nouns
the **waiter's** tray	**men's** ties
the **shoemaker's** tools	**sisters-in-law's** agreement
Dean **Kloss's** contract	the **Williamses'** pool
my **brother-in-law's** cars	my **sisters'** bedroom

A Write the possessive form of the noun in parentheses to complete each sentence.

1. _____ name may not mean much to you. **(G. W. G. Ferris)**

2. Yet you probably enjoy one of this _____ creations. **(inventor)**

3. _____ eyes still light up at the sight of one. **(People)**

4. Its _____ excited squeals tell you what fun it is. **(passengers)**

5. The _____ gasps can be heard when they reach the top. **(riders)**

6. The Ferris wheel is a _____ main attraction. **(fairground)**

B 7–12. This encyclopedia entry has six incorrect or missing apostrophes. Use proofreading marks to correct the entry.

Example: The Ferris wheel at the World's Columbian Exposition in Chicago in 1893 was the largest ever built.

Proofreading Marks
- ¶ Indent
- ∧ Add
- ⌒ Delete
- ≡ Capital letter
- / Small letter
- ՞՞ Add quotes
- ∧ Add comma
- ⊙ Add period
- ∪ Transpose

Proofreading

A world's fair is an international exposition. The first worlds' fair was Londons Great Exhibition of 1851. Since then, more than 80 fairs have been held throughout the world.

Fairs have been a showcase for many inventor's new products. Alexander Graham Bells' telephone was displayed at Philadelphias Centennial Exhibition in 1876. St. Louis' Exposition in 1904 featured new foods like the ice-cream cone.

(continued)

Grade 7: Unit 2 Nouns (Use with pupil book pages 81–83.)
Skill: Students will form singular and plural possessive nouns.

Grammar/Mechanics

Name _____

4 Possessive Nouns (continued from page 27)

Challenge

Solve these riddles. The answer to each riddle is made up of one plural noun and one possessive noun. Both nouns rhyme.

Example: the clothing of some insects   ants' pants

1. the pastimes of a boy named Robby   _____

2. headgear for purring animals   _____

3. pieces of furniture owned by Mabel   _____

4. buckets of some mammals   _____

5. linens of a wise bird   _____

6. equipment of a silly person   _____

7. the customs of some animals   _____

8. vessels belonging to certain four-legged animals   _____

Now make up two riddles of your own. Be sure to include a singular or a plural possessive noun in the answer to each riddle.

                 RIDDLES   **ANSWERS**

9. _____   _____

10. _____   _____

Writing Application: Sentence —

We often admire many different people. Perhaps you admire your sister's courage and your friends' musical talents. Write five sentences that tell about special qualities you admire in different people you know. Use a possessive noun in each sentence.

Revising Strategies: Sentence Fluency

Writing with Possessive Nouns

Simple sentences	The bowling alley has Thursday night specials. The Thursday night specials help increase business.
Combined sentence	**The bowling alley's Thursday night specials** help increase business.

Combining Sentences 1–5. Revise the description. Use possessive nouns to combine the underlined pairs of sentences.

Revising

Bowling ranks among the top participant sports in the world. The game was organized in the United States in 1875. The rules, however, varied from place to place until 1895. The American Bowling Congress drew up the official rules. These are the rules we play by today.

There are standards for alley size and ball size. The alley must be a specific width. This width must be 41 to 42 inches. No variations are allowed. The alley must be a specific length. The length must be 60 feet from the foul line to the center of the head pin. The approach to the foul line must be at least 15 feet. The bowler has the ability to take several running steps before releasing the ball. This ability provides the needed momentum. The largest circumference that the ball can be is 27 inches. The ball has a certain weight limit. This weight limit is no more than 16 pounds.

1. _____

2. _____

3. _____

4. _____

5. _____

(continued)

Grade 7: Unit 2 Nouns *(Use with pupil book pages 84–85.)*
Skill: Students will use possessive nouns to combine sentences.

Revising Strategies: Sentence Fluency

Name _____

Writing with Possessive Nouns (continued from page 29)

Wordy sentence	I never understood the sense of humor that belongs to my older brother.
More concise sentence	I never understood **my older brother's sense of humor**.

Writing Concise Sentences 6–10. Revise the description. Use possessive nouns to make each underlined sentence more concise.

Revising

The students in my class are unique. The class is always interesting because of the special talent that each student possesses.

For example, I am always impressed by the intelligence of Jason. No matter what topic we discuss, Jason has the answer to the most difficult of questions. The rest of the class depends on the insight and broad knowledge that belong to Jason. Of course, Keisha brings her own brand of uniqueness to the class.

The jokes that Keisha tells never fail to lift the spirits of everyone. She always seems to have the perfect anecdote or quip for the occasion.

The teachers allow me to demonstrate my particular talent only during lunch or recess. At first I was not sure that anyone would even notice my ability to wiggle my ears. However, the applause that is given by my classmates confirms both their approval and their enjoyment.

6. _____
7. _____
8. _____
9. _____
10. _____

Revising Strategies: Vocabulary

Exact Nouns

The ~~worker~~ cashier mistakenly overcharged Jenna for the ~~clothing~~ pants.

1–10. Replace each underlined weak noun with a more exact one from the box. Be sure the noun you choose fits the meaning of the sentence.

store	news	sweaters
slippers	breakfast	restaurant
things	waitress	outfits
bus	Roosevelt Shopping Center	cereal
refreshment	booth	drink
owner	coats	sneakers
airplane	schedule	

Revising

A trip to the <u>mall</u> is always exciting for Jenna. She loves buying new <u>items</u> to wear at the start of the school year. Today Jenna leaves home early in the morning. Before she begins shopping, she decides to get <u>a meal</u>. She goes to the <u>place</u> and orders <u>food</u>. The <u>worker</u> serves her quickly, and Jenna is off to shop.

There are so many stores to visit that it is difficult for Jenna to decide where to begin. Finally, she enters Walter's Department Store. There she purchases three <u>tops</u> that will go perfectly with the new pants she bought last week. Next she goes to the shoe store. There she purchases a pair of <u>shoes</u> for gym class. Jenna spends the rest of the afternoon window-shopping. At 5 o'clock she decides to leave. She hopes to catch the early <u>vehicle</u> so that she can get home in time to watch the <u>program</u> on television.

Grade 7: Unit 2 Nouns *(Use with pupil book page 86.)*
Skill: Students will replace weak nouns with exact nouns.

Grammar/Mechanics

Name _____

1 Kinds of Verbs

Action verbs	Many people **have wondered** about ostriches.
	Ostriches **look** for plants, lizards, and turtles.
Being verbs	They **look** unusual. (linking verb)
	Ostriches **are** the largest birds in the world. (linking verb)
	More information about them **is** in the encyclopedia.

A Write the verb in each sentence. Then label it *action* or *being*.

1. Ostriches roam the plains of East Africa. _____
2. The ostrich is one of the fastest animals alive. _____
3. It can run faster than a horse. _____
4. Its feet are very strong. _____
5. It uses them for defense. _____
6. Ostriches see very well. _____
7. Many people believe a myth about ostriches. _____
8. The myth is not true. _____
9. An ostrich does not bury its head in the sand. _____
10. Ostriches eat many kinds of plants. _____
11. They can live as long as seventy years. _____

B Write the verb in each sentence. Then label it *action* or *linking*.

12. Have you ever felt an ostrich's feathers? _____
13. They feel soft and fluffy. _____
14. They look beautiful. _____
15. Women once appeared at parties in ostrich-feather hats. _____
16. These hats became the style in the 1800s. _____

(continued)

WORKBOOK PLUS Grade 7: Unit 3 Verbs *(Use with pupil book pages 100–103.)*
Skill: Students will identify action and being verbs.

Grammar/Mechanics   Name _____

1 Kinds of Verbs (continued from page 32)

Challenge

You are a TV announcer for a program about unusual animals. On this afternoon's show, you will be discussing the ostrich, the sloth, the angler, and the narwhal. Write one sentence you will say about each animal. In each sentence use a verb that expresses mental action, physical action, or a state of being.

You Say: _____   You Say: _____
_____   _____
_____   _____

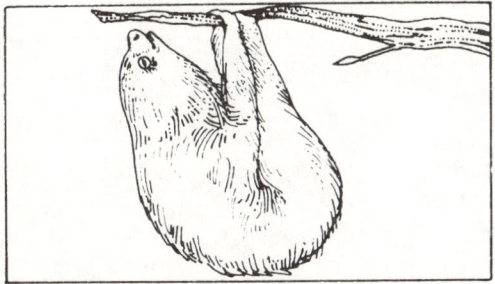

You Say: _____   You Say: _____
_____   _____
_____   _____

Writing Application: A Scientific Report ————————————

Suppose that you are a biologist. You have just discovered a new kind of animal. Write a short report that describes how the animal looks, sounds, and behaves. Include verbs that express physical action, mental action, and a state of being.

Grade 7: Unit 3 Verbs (Use with pupil book pages 100–103.)
Skill: Students will use action and being verbs.

Grammar/Mechanics

2 Verb Phrases

```
       auxiliary        main
          |              |
People have always worried about the weather.
  auxiliary                   main
     |                          |
Aren't weather forecasts improving?
                  auxiliary main
                      |      |
Satellite forecasts can be very accurate.
```

Write the verb phrase in each sentence. Then underline the main verb.

1. Our class has been studying the monsoons of southern Asia. _____

2. Have you ever heard of these special winds? _____

3. In winter, monsoons will blow from land to sea. _____

4. The weather can become very dry during this time. _____

5. In summer these winds will travel from sea to land. _____

6. The summer monsoons will usually bring rain. _____

7. One Indian city has recorded eleven meters of rain in one year. _____

8. Scientists still don't fully understand monsoons. _____

9. In some years monsoons have arrived very early or very late. _____

10. The summer rainfall is anticipated with both hope and fear by many people. _____

11. Too much rain can cause floods and erosion. _____

12. Too little rain may result in a drought. _____

13. A summer without rain does not help farmers. _____

14. With luck the summer monsoons should bring welcome rain this year. _____

(continued)

34 WORKBOOK PLUS

Grade 7: Unit 3 Verbs (Use with pupil book pages 104–106.)
Skill: Students will identify verb phrases and main verbs.

Grammar/Mechanics

2 Verb Phrases (continued from page 34)

Challenge

TV weather reporter Stormy Wethers is famous for doing two things. She always gives forecasts that are incorrect, and she always tells terrible jokes when she's on the air.

"Good evening. I guess you <u>may have noticed</u> something by now. The sun is not <u>shining</u> as I <u>had predicted</u>."

The picture above shows Stormy at her weather map. Write a joke that Stormy might tell before her forecast. Use a verb phrase in your joke.

Stormy's Joke: _____

_____

_____

Now write Stormy's forecast for tomorrow's weather and her long-range predictions for the coming week. Use a verb phrase in each sentence.

Stormy's Forecast: _____

_____

_____

Stormy's Long-range Predictions: _____

_____

_____

Writing Application: A Post Card

Suppose that you are vacationing in a wonderful place. Write a post card to a friend. Describe the weather at your vacation spot, and try to convince your friend to join you. Use verb phrases in five of your sentences.

Grade 7: Unit 3 Verbs (Use with pupil book pages 104–106.)
Skill: Students will use verb phrases in sentences.

Grammar/Mechanics

3 Simple Verb Tenses

Present Tense	Past Tense	Future Tense
Jan **prepares** a salad.	Jan **prepared** a salad.	Jan **will prepare** a salad.
She **chops** celery.	She **chopped** celery.	She **will chop** celery.
She **tries** the dressing.	She **tried** the dressing.	She **will try** the dressing.

Complete each sentence with the tense of the verb shown in parentheses.

1. The history club's pioneer feast _____ in one hour. (**start—future**)

2. The group _____ a special kind of stew called burgoo. (**serve—future**)

3. Pioneers in Kentucky _____ this stew. (**invent—past**)

4. Many club members _____ with the preparations. (**help—past**)

5. Some students _____ potatoes for the stew. (**peel—past**)

6. Others _____ the meat and the vegetables. (**chop—past**)

7. The club president _____ while slicing onions. (**cry—past**)

8. Elliot and Vivian _____ the stew frequently. (**stir—past**)

9. They also _____ it a few times. (**taste—past**)

10. They _____ for more than one helping tonight. (**hope—present**)

11. Now Elliot _____ all the dirty pots and pans. (**wash—present**)

12. Vivian _____ them quickly. (**dry—present**)

13. She _____ the clean dishes to Louis to put away. (**pass—present**)

14. Soon they _____ cleaning up the kitchen. (**finish—future**)

15. At tomorrow's club meeting, they _____ their next banquet. (**plan—future**)

(continued)

Grade 7: Unit 3 Verbs (Use with pupil book pages 107–109.)
Skill: Students will form the present, past, and future tenses of verbs.

Grammar/Mechanics

3 Simple Verb Tenses (continued from page 36)

Challenge

The four pictures below show some of the things that Mai Moran does each day. Write a sentence to describe each of Mai's activities. Imagine that it is now 6:00 P.M. Use the past tense to describe what Mai did before 6:00 P.M. Use the present tense to describe what Mai does at 6:00 P.M. Use the future tense to describe what Mai will do after 6:00 P.M.

Now number the pictures in the order that the actions occur. Write the numbers in the small boxes.

Writing Application: A Story — INFORMING

Suppose that you have invented an amazing new food. Tell how you created this food. Describe the effects of the new food on someone who is eating it now. Tell how you plan to let the world know about this tasty item.

Grade 7: Unit 3 Verbs (Use with pupil book pages 107–109.)
Skill: Students will use verbs in the present, past, and future tenses.

WORKBOOK PLUS 37

Grammar/Usage

Name _____

4 be, have, and do

Subjects	Forms of *be*	Forms of *have*	Forms of *do*
I	am, was	have, had	do, did
he, she, it	is, was	has, had	does, did
singular nouns	is, was	has, had	does, did
we, you, they	are, were	have, had	do, did
plural nouns	are, were	have, had	do, did

A Complete each sentence with the form of the verb shown in parentheses.

1. I _____ doing a report on the potato. (**be—present**)

2. Potatoes _____ root vegetables. (**be—present**)

3. They _____ first grown in South America. (**be—past**)

4. Europeans _____ not like potatoes at first. (**do—past**)

5. By the 1800s potatoes _____ become a major crop in parts of Europe. (**have—past**)

B 6–14. This ad has nine incorrect verb forms. Use proofreading marks to correct the ad.

Example: Is potatoes good for you? *(Are)*

Proofreading Marks
- ¶ Indent
- ∧ Add
- ⌒ Delete
- ≡ Capital letter
- / Small letter
- ⌄⌄ Add quotes
- ∧ Add comma
- ⊙ Add period
- ⌣ Transpose

Proofreading

The Potato—See What It Do for You!

Is you feeling tired?

Potatoes has vitamins and proteins to put a spring in your step!

Does you want to shed a few pounds?

An average potato have only a hundred calories.

Be you looking for a way to cut down on fat?

Potatoes is not just low-fat; they has NO fat.

POTATOES—the good-tasting, fast-energy, no-fat, low-cal food! Have you has your potato today?

(continued)

38 WORKBOOK PLUS

Grade 7: Unit 3 Verbs (*Use with pupil book pages 110–112.*)
Skill: Students will form the present and past tenses of *be*, *have*, and *do*.

Grammar/Usage

Name _____

4 be, have, and do (continued from page 38)

Challenge

Many funny jokes and riddles have been written about vegetables. How many do you know? Complete each question with the correct form of the verb in parentheses.

1. What _____ the vegetables say when it was time to get started? (do—past)   _____ cauliflower

2. Which vegetable _____ a name like a dog in bloom? (have—present)   _____ eggplant

3. What vegetables _____ like the sound of a drum? (be—present)   _____ "I yam what I yam."

4. What _____ the favorite statement of a sailor in cartoons? (be—present)   _____ "Lettuce begin."

5. What kind of vegetable _____ laid by a bird? (be—past)   _____ potatoes

6. What vegetables _____ eyes but cannot see? (have—present)   _____ beets

7. What _____ an unkind vegetable say to someone it disliked? (do—past)   _____ leeks

8. What vegetables _____ sunk many boats? (have—present)   _____ "I don't carrot all for you."

Now match each question with the correct answer. Write the number of the question on the line next to the answer.

Writing Application: A Recipe

Suppose that you and a friend have just created a delicious new vegetable soup. You decide to write down the recipe so that you can make the soup again at a later time. Write several sentences, describing how you made this one-of-a-kind dish. Use at least three forms of *be*, *have*, and *do* in your recipe.

Grade 7: Unit 3 Verbs (Use with pupil book pages 110–112.)
Skill: Students will write the present and past tenses of *be*, *have*, and *do*.

Grammar/Usage

5 Perfect Tenses

Verb	Present Participle	Past	Past Participle
exercise	(is) exercising	exercised	(has) exercised
hop	(is) hopping	hopped	(has) hopped
try	(is) trying	tried	(has) tried
Present perfect tense	Irene **has exercised** today.		
	Her sisters **have exercised** today too.		
Past perfect tense	Irene **had exercised** before.		
Future perfect tense	Irene **will have exercised** by 5:00 P.M.		

A Write the tense of each underlined verb.

1. Our class <u>has started</u> a new fitness program. _____
2. Before we did, we <u>had scored</u> low on fitness tests. _____
3. Most of us <u>have improved</u> after just three weeks. _____
4. By the end of the year, we <u>will have strengthened</u> our muscles. _____
5. We <u>will have discovered</u> new ways to stay fit. _____
6. I wish I <u>had tried</u> this sooner. _____

B Write the principal parts of each verb.

	Verb	Present Participle	Past	Past Participle
7.	tap	_____	_____	_____
8.	tape	_____	_____	_____
9.	hurry	_____	_____	_____
10.	play	_____	_____	_____
11.	slam	_____	_____	_____
12.	notice	_____	_____	_____
13.	swim	_____	_____	_____
14.	jog	_____	_____	_____

(continued)

Grammar/Usage

Name _____

5 Perfect Tenses *(continued from page 40)*

Challenge

You are a television sportscaster, covering the Falmouth Marathon. The race began at 8:00 A.M., and Luis Romero immediately took the lead. At 9:35 the camera cuts to you for your report. Using the map below, describe Luis's progress so far and how you expect him to perform in the remainder of the race. Use a verb in the perfect tense in each sentence of your commentary.

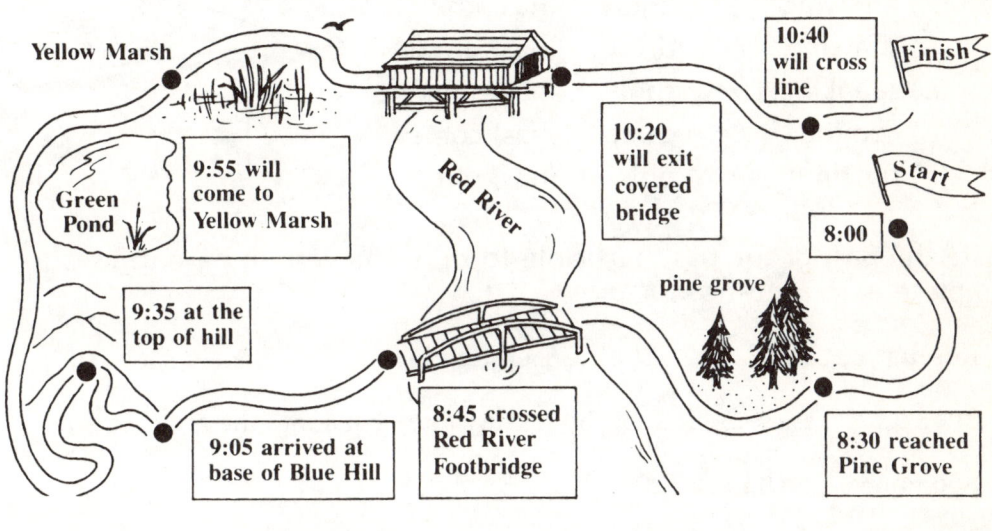

_____
_____
_____
_____
_____
_____
_____
_____

Writing Application: A Letter

Suppose that you exercise at a gym each day. A fitness instructor has planned a fitness program for you. Write a letter to a friend, describing the kinds of exercises that you do at the gym. Include verbs in the perfect tenses in your letter.

Grade 7: Unit 3 Verbs *(Use with pupil book pages 113–116.)*
Skill: Students will use the perfect tenses.

Grammar/Usage

Name _____

6 Irregular Verbs

Verb	Present Participle	Past	Past Participle
be	(is) being	was	(has) been
have	(is) having	had	(has) had
do	(is) doing	did	(has) done
begin	(is) beginning	began	(has) begun
tear	(is) tearing	tore	(has) torn
know	(is) knowing	knew	(has) known
draw	(is) drawing	drew	(has) drawn
speak	(is) speaking	spoke	(has) spoken
come	(is) coming	came	(has) come
put	(is) putting	put	(has) put

A Write the past or the past participle form of the verb in parentheses to complete each sentence.

1. Rosetta _____ her juggling act at our talent show. **(do)**

2. She _____ by tossing three balls into the air. **(begin)**

3. Soon one of the balls _____. **(fall)**

4. "I should have _____ that would happen," she said. **(know)**

5. "They've _____ their ups and downs all day." **(have)**

B 6–10. This review article has five errors with irregular verbs. Use proofreading marks to correct the article.

Example: Dan stood on his head and ~~throwed~~ threw 11 coins into a jar.

Proofreading Marks
- ¶ Indent
- ∧ Add
- ℘ Delete
- ≡ Capital letter
- / Small letter
- ʾʾ ʾʾ Add quotes
- ∧ Add comma
- ⊙ Add period
- ∽ Transpose

Proofreading

Millerton Middle School put on a talent show Friday night. The students done a great job. Everyone had knowed the tumbling routine by Darryl Jones and Amy Chu would be a success. Then somebody speak poetry in a soft voice while the lights were still low. No one have any idea who the student was. Then a spotlight come on, and we saw that the speaker was Maria Alonzo's mynah bird!

(continued)

Grade 7: Unit 3 Verbs (Use with pupil book pages 117–119.)
Skill: Students will form the past and the past participle forms of irregular verbs.

Grammar/Usage

6 Irregular Verbs (continued from page 42)

Challenge

Last night you attended a play at a local theater. You enjoyed the play so much that you quickly wrote a letter of praise to the director of the theater group. In your excitement you used many incorrect verb forms in your letter. Cross out each incorrect past or past participle form, and write the correct verb form above it.

Dear Director,

　　Last night I choosed to attend a play putted on by your theater group. Once the play had began, I realized that I had came to see a wonderful performance. Act I was so suspenseful! By the time the curtain come down, I had simply freezed in my chair. I also liked the comedy scene in Act II, in which the actor fighted with the lid of a spaghetti sauce jar.

　　After Act II had drew to a close, I speaked to the person in the next seat. She said she had shook with fright during Act I. She had also nearly fell off her chair during the spaghetti sauce scene.

　　After the play I teared home to write this letter. Thank you for a delightful evening!

　　　　　　　　　　　　　　　　　　　　　　Sincerely,

　　　　　　　　　　　　　　　　　　　　　　_____

Now imagine that you are the director of the local theater group who received this letter of praise. On a separate piece of paper, write a reply to the letter. Use at least five irregular verbs from this lesson.

Writing Application: A Letter

Suppose that you have ordered a costume from a mail-order catalog, but you are not satisfied with it. Write a letter of complaint to the company. Explain why you are returning the costume. Use the past or the past participle form of at least five verbs from the box below.

shrink	come	begin	tear	do	put	have	do

Grade 7: Unit 3　Verbs　(Use with pupil book pages 117–119.)
Skill: Students will use the past and the past participle forms of irregular verbs.

WORKBOOK PLUS
43

Grammar/Usage

7 More Irregular Verbs

Verb	Present Participle	Past	Past Participle
go	(is) going	went	(has) gone
give	(is) giving	gave	(has) given
get	(is) getting	got	(has) gotten
lose	(is) losing	lost	(has) lost
ride	(is) riding	rode	(has) ridden
say	(is) saying	said	(has) said
see	(is) seeing	saw	(has) seen
sell	(is) selling	sold	(has) sold
think	(is) thinking	thought	(has) thought

A Write the past or the past participle form of the verb in parentheses to complete each sentence.

1. Stephanie has _____ her old bicycle. **(sell)**

2. She has _____ a new ten-speed bike. **(get)**

3. She _____ it at her favorite bicycle shop. **(buy)**

4. At first she _____ all the bikes were too expensive. **(think)**

5. She finally _____ one that she could afford. **(see)**

B 6–10. This ad has five errors with the past tenses of irregular verbs. Use proofreading marks to correct the ad.

Example: Yesterday in gym class Marcus tell̂ me that he wants a new Traveler mountain bike.

Proofreading Marks
- ¶ Indent
- ∧ Add
- ◡ Delete
- ≡ Capital letter
- / Small letter
- ˇˇ Add quotes
- ⌃ Add comma
- ⊙ Add period
- ∽ Transpose

Proofreading

Traveler Mountain Bikes Are Best For Students!

Have you went bike riding lately? Has your old bike gave you trouble? Have you think of buying a new bike? If you have ever rode a mountain bike down a country road, you should give the Traveler a try.

In road tests last year, students in Utah give the Traveler an AAA rating.

(continued)

Grammar/Usage

Name _____

7 More Irregular Verbs (continued from page 44)

Challenge

You are participating in a five-day bicycle tour. It's been a hard ride. After twenty-five miles, your group stops for a rest. You write a post card to your parents, omitting some past and past participle verb forms. Complete each sentence with the correct form of each verb from the picture below.

Dear Mom and Dad,

We have already _____ twenty-five miles. I have

_____ no speed records. In the morning one of my pedals

_____ the edge of a curb, and I almost _____

my balance. I had already _____ a lot of time when I

_____ a flat tire. I probably would have _____

better time if I had _____ all the way! My companions had

_____ so far ahead of me that I forgot my way. When I finally

_____ up with them, they had already _____

lunch. Would you be upset if I _____ my bicycle and

_____ home?

Love,

_____

Writing Application: A Good Beginning — NARRATING

Write a beginning for a short story called "The Great Bicycle Escape." You may write it as a science-fiction story, a fairy tale, or a realistic suspense story. Use a principal part of at least four verbs from the box below.

| drink | feel | break | ride | see | drive | think | sing |

Grade 7: Unit 3 Verbs (Use with pupil book pages 120–123.)
Skill: Students will use the past and the past participle forms of irregular verbs.

8 Progressive Forms

Present progressive	Kyoko **is picking** wildflowers on her farm.
Past progressive	She **was picking** them when I called her.
Future progressive	She **will be picking** more later.
Present perfect progressive	She **has been picking** lavender flowers.
Past perfect progressive	She **had been picking** blue ones earlier.
Future perfect progressive	She **will have been picking** for an hour by the time I get there.

A Write the progressive verb form in each sentence. Then write the name of the form.

1. Kyoko and I have been collecting wildflowers.
   _____

2. Today we are drying the flowers. _____

3. Some of them are hanging upside-down in my barn.
   _____

B 4–8. This postcard has five errors with progressive forms of verbs. Use proofreading marks to correct the postcard.

Example: Today many cooks ^are^ using herbs to add flavor to food.

Proofreading

I'm having a great vacation. My aunt teaching me about wildflowers and herbs. She been using herbs for cooking and healing for many years. When you called, I picking marigold leaves to make a cream for sunburns. This afternoon we will making tea from raspberry leaves. I had been want to learn about herbs for a long time.

Love, Lynn

Proofreading Marks
¶ Indent
∧ Add
⌒ Delete
≡ Capital letter
/ Small letter
⌄⌄ Add quotes
∧ Add comma
⊙ Add period
∽ Transpose

(continued)

Grammar/Usage

Name _____

8 Progressive Forms (continued from page 46)

Challenge

Millicent Pembroke, Private Investigator, is working on a difficult case. A valuable orchid has been stolen. Help Millicent solve the case. Complete each of the sentences in her log. Use a progressive form of each verb from the orchids below.

report, call, rain, hold, search, demand, pound, develop, ring, expect, await, stand

I _____ outside the phone booth for an hour. It _____ the entire time. I _____ a call from my assistant, Boris Bloodhound. He _____ every flower show and florist shop in the metropolitan area for the missing orchid. Any minute now he _____ to report his findings.

Obviously the owner of this valuable plant _____ the results of Bloodhound's investigation too. Sir Horty Culture _____ this unusual orchid for years. He thinks that Willy Dewitt, his chief competitor, _____ the orchid for ransom.

At last my phone _____! My heart _____! _____ Bloodhound _____ that "The Case of the Missing Orchid" is solved or _____ a blackmailer _____ a fortune? TO BE CONTINUED...

Writing Application: A Diary Entry

Suppose that you raise flowers. You are sitting in a spot that overlooks your fields. Write a page in your diary, describing what you are seeing and feeling. Tell what you have done today and what you plan to do tomorrow. Include at least five progressive verb forms.

Grade 7: Unit 3 Verbs (Use with pupil book pages 124–126.)
Skill: Students will use progressive verb forms correctly.

WORKBOOK PLUS 47

Revising Strategies: Sentence Fluency

Writing with Verbs

Incorrect tense	Last week we go to the museum, and we saw the dinosaur exhibit.
Correct tense	Last week we **went** to the museum, and we saw the dinosaur exhibit.

Using Tenses Consistently 1–6. Revise the paragraph. Use each verb in the correct tense.

Revising

Dinosaurs roam the earth sometime between 250 and 65 million years ago. This period was known as the time of the deinos ("terrible") sauros ("lizard"). These animals rule the earth for about 140 million years. The first dinosaurs study by scientists were the Megalosaurus and Iguanodon. Their partial bones were found early in the 19th century in England. By the early 20th century new kinds of dinosaurs are discovered around the world. During the time of the dinosaur, the Earth is vastly different than it is today. Back then, the Earth has higher surface temperatures and only one large land mass as opposed to separate continents. As a result, dinosaur fossils have been found in all parts of the globe.

(continued)

Grade 7: Unit 3 Verbs *(Use with pupil book pages 127–128.)*
Skill: Students will use consistent tenses in their writing.

Revising Strategies: Sentence Fluency

Name _____

Writing with Verbs (continued from page 48)

Incorrect tense	Donna has been stationed on the Martian outpost since March and was relieved next Saturday.
Correct tense	Donna has been stationed on the Martian outpost since March and **will be** relieved next Saturday.

Telling Exactly When 7–14. Revise the description. Use the correct tense to tell exactly when each event occurred.

Revising

   For the past two months Donna is gathering data about Martian dust storms. Many of these storms originate in the deep basins of Mars' southern hemisphere. Martian dust storms will not be like those on Earth. The dust was a fine silt, almost like flour, that swirls in winds that approach 50 to 60 miles per hour. Sometimes the storms are intense and dust covered the face of the entire planet. If such a storm starts now, Donna did not leave Mars tomorrow, as scheduled. Fortunately, the winds are out of the east at a mere 6 miles per hour, and it seems unlikely they changed overnight.

   Donna has already packed for her return trip and was waiting to hear from her commander. The call comes through. The shuttle is on course and arrived on time.

Grade 7: Unit 3 Verbs (Use with pupil book pages 127–128.)
Skill: Students will use verbs in the correct tense to tell exactly when events occur.

Grammar/Usage

Name _____

9 Transitive and Intransitive Verbs

Transitive Verbs	Intransitive Verbs
Maureen **served** the ball.	Maureen **had served** and **volleyed** well.
She **defeated** her easily.	She **was** the best player on the court.

Write each verb. Then label it *transitive* or *intransitive*.

1. In 1874 a woman from the United States watched some British soldiers in Bermuda.

   _____

2. The soldiers were holding rackets and were hitting a little ball back and forth over a net.

   _____

3. This woman, Mary Outerbridge, learned about the game.

   _____

4. She returned to the United States and told her brother about it.

   _____

5. Her brother, Emilius Outerbridge, directed a sports club on Staten Island in New York City.

6. Emilius became enthusiastic about tennis too.

   _____

7. He built a tennis court at his club.

   _____

8. The sport grew popular, and tennis courts appeared in many cities.

   _____

9. In 1881 Emilius Outerbridge and two other men formed the United States National Lawn Tennis Association. _____

10. This association held its first championship in Newport, Rhode Island, in that same year.

    _____

(continued)

Grammar/Usage

Name _____

9 Transitive and Intransitive Verbs (continued from page 50)

Challenge

Your friend Jeanette is a runner, and you're her manager. She is entering a ten kilometer race on March 27, and you have devised a training schedule for her. Write a short article for your local newspaper, explaining Jeanette's training program. Use transitive and intransitive verbs. Underline each transitive verb once and each intransitive verb twice.

March

Sunday	Monday	Tuesday	Wednesday	Thursday	Friday	Saturday
	1 swim laps	2	3 run in park	4	5	6 run in park
7 rest	8 lift weights	9	10 run in park	11	12 play basketball	13 run in park
14 rest	15 lift weights	16	17 run in park	18	19 aerobics	20 run in park
21 rest	22 swim laps	23 aerobics	24 run in park	25	26 spaghetti dinner	27 ENTER RACE
28	29	30	31			

_____
_____
_____
_____
_____
_____

Writing Application: An Article

Write a short magazine article that tells readers how to select a specific piece of sports equipment. You might write about choosing a tennis racket or selecting exercise equipment. Use transitive and intransitive verbs in your article. Underline each transitive verb and circle each intransitive verb.

Grade 7: Unit 3 Verbs (Use with pupil book pages 129–131.)
Skill: Students will use transitive and intransitive verbs.

Grammar/Usage Name _____

10 Direct and Indirect Objects

>   indirect   direct   direct
> Elsa told **me** some strange **facts** about insects called **cicadas**.
>   direct   direct
> She observed **cicadas** and **katydids** in her back yard.
>   indirect   indirect direct
> She told her **teacher** and her **classmates facts** about insects.
>   indirect   direct
> The teacher gave her **report** a high **grade**.

Write each object. Then label it *direct* or *indirect*.

1. A female cicada finds a tree or a shrub.
_____

2. The insect drills a hole in a twig and lays its eggs.
_____

3. A hatched cicada digs a home in the ground. _____

4. Finally, it climbs a tree and sheds its skin.
_____

5. Elsa took us to her house. _____

6. She showed Joel and me her drawings of cicadas.
_____

7. The next day Elsa played a tape of cicada songs for our class.
_____

8. We gave the songs our undivided attention.
_____

9. Some students asked Elsa questions.
_____

10. Our teacher gave her the highest grade in the class.
_____

(continued)

Grammar/Usage

Name _____

10 Direct and Indirect Objects (continued from page 52)

Challenge

Mariko has taken wonderful photographs of insects. Below are the names of some of the insects she has photographed. Use each insect name to help you write a sentence. Each important word in your sentence must begin with one of the letters in the insect's name. Follow the pattern in parentheses. First, read these sentence patterns.

```
   SVD   = subject + verb + direct object
  SVID   = subject + verb + indirect object + direct object
 SVIIDD  = subject + verb + indirect object + indirect object +
           direct object + direct object
```

Example: BUG (SVD) = Belinda understands geography.

BEE (SVD) = _____

ANT (SVD) = _____

FLY (SVD) = _____

WASP (SVID) = _____

MOTH (SVID) = _____

HORNET (SVIIDD) = _____

CICADA (SVIIDD) = _____

Writing Application: An Article ———————————————— INFORMING

You have been asked by a children's magazine to write a short article. You decide to write an article about interesting hobbies for young children. Include direct and indirect objects in your article. Underline each direct object once and each indirect object twice.

Grade 7: Unit 3 Verbs (Use with pupil book pages 132–135.)
Skill: Students will write sentences, using direct and indirect objects.

11 Predicate Nouns and Predicate Adjectives

| Predicate noun | John Steinbeck is the **author** of *The Red Pony*. |
| Predicate adjectives | The story seems **realistic** and **sad**. |

Write the predicate nouns and predicate adjectives.
Then label them *predicate noun* or *predicate adjective*.

1. One of my favorite books is *The Red Pony*.

2. Jody Tiflin is the main character in *The Red Pony*.

3. The pony is a gift from Jody's father.

4. Jody is always careful and gentle with his pony.

5. At one point in the story the pony becomes very ill.

6. Jody feels sad and angry about his pony's illness.

7. Billy Buck is Jody's friend and a worker on the farm.

8. Billy had been the trainer of Jody's pony earlier in the story.

9. He feels responsible for the pony's sickness.

10. Because of his many experiences, Jody grows more mature.

(continued)

Grammar/Usage

Name _____

11 Predicate Nouns and Predicate Adjectives (continued from page 54)

Challenge

Andrea is writing a report about five famous authors. She has used the biographies shown below for her notes. Match each book title with the correct set of notes. Then write the underlined letter from each title in the blank next to the correct set of notes.

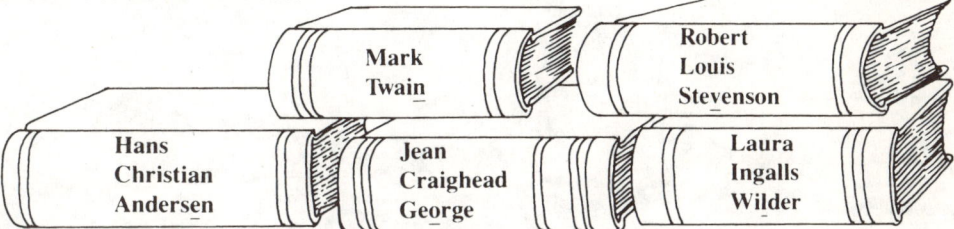

NOTES

1. Created Tom Sawyer and Huckleberry Finn, humorous _____
2. Nature subjects, *Julie of the Wolves, My Side of the Mountain* _____
3. Scottish, poet, adventure stories, *Treasure Island* _____
4. Fairy-tale writer, Danish, an ugly duckling _____
5. Series of books, *Little House on the Prairie* _____

Your answers are correct if the letters you have written are a synonym for *book*. Now write the notes as sentences. Each sentence must contain a predicate noun or a predicate adjective.

6. _____
7. _____
8. _____
9. _____
10. _____

Writing Application: A Description ————————————

Write a paragraph about your favorite character. Describe the character's appearance, feelings, and thoughts. Include predicate nouns and predicate adjectives in your paragraph. Underline each predicate noun once and each predicate adjective twice.

Grammar/Usage

12 Active and Passive Voices

Active voice	The Dutch **named** the continent New Holland.
Passive voice	The continent **was named** New Holland by the Dutch.

Write *active* or *passive* to describe the verb in each sentence. If the verb is active, rewrite the sentence using a passive verb. If it is passive, rewrite the sentence using an active verb.

1. The Aborigines inhabited Australia for thousands of years. _____

2. Captain James Cook, an Englishman, visited Australia in 1770. _____

3. Cook explored Botany Bay and most of Australia's east coast. _____

4. The bay was named by Cook. _____

5. Kangaroos and other animals were found by the explorers. _____

6. The Great Barrier Reef was also discovered by Cook. _____

7. The reef nearly destroyed Cook's ship. _____

8. The new land was claimed by Cook for England. _____

(continued)

Grade 7: Unit 3 Verbs (Use with pupil book pages 139–141.)
Skill: Students will identify and will write active and passive verbs.

Grammar/Usage

Name _____

12 Active and Passive Voices (continued from page 56)

Challenge

Sheila is making an outline of important historical events. She has already made a list of explorers and a list of places that they discovered. Unfortunately she does not know who discovered what. Help Sheila by matching a name from Column A with an event from Column B. Write the correct letter on the line next to the event.

COLUMN A		COLUMN B
o. Coronado	_____	Settlements in "Vinland" are established
r. Daniel Boone	_____	China is reached by an overland route
i. Marco Polo	_____	New World is discovered
v. Ponce de Leon	_____	The Pacific Ocean is located
d. Vikings	_____	Southwestern United States is explored
y. Lewis and Clark	_____	"Fountain of Youth" is sought
s. Columbus	_____	Plymouth Colony is settled
c. Balboa	_____	Settlers are brought to Kentucky
e. Pilgrims	_____	Louisiana Purchase is explored

Your answers are correct if the letters you have written spell a word that means "a finding." Now, on a separate piece of paper, write each group of words in Column B as a sentence. Each sentence must include the name of an explorer and a verb in the active voice.

Writing Application: A Paragraph — NARRATING

Write a paragraph about a place that you and your family have explored. Describe the place and tell what you did and saw there. Use only verbs in the active voice. Then rewrite your paragraph, changing all the verbs to passive voice.

Grade 7: Unit 3 Verbs (Use with pupil book pages 139–141.)
Skill: Students will write sentences, using active and passive verbs.

WORKBOOK PLUS 57

Revising Strategies: Sentence Fluency

Writing with Verbs

Passive voice	The polar bear **is observed and enjoyed** by visitors at the zoo.
Active voice	Visitors at the zoo **observe and enjoy** the polar bear.

Writing Clearly with the Active Voice 1–5. Revise the paragraph. Change each underlined sentence to the active voice.

Revising

The sea ice of the North Polar Basin is roamed by an intelligent animal. With a weight that can exceed 1000 pounds, the brilliant white polar bear is truly a majestic beast. A varied diet of kelp, mussels, berries, seal, and fish is eaten by the bears. They have little interest in any Arctic species that is not on their menu. Humans who are foolish enough to approach them are often ignored by the bears. The female polar bear is an excellent candidate for mother-of-the-year award. A strong bond is formed by female bears with their young. At birth these bears weigh less than 2 pounds. For the first 40 days the baby bear is tended to and kept warm by the mother bear. Because polar bears live in such a remote environment, the bear population has remained stable.

1. _____

2. _____

3. _____

4. _____

5. _____

(continued)

Revising Strategies: Sentence Fluency

Name _____

Writing with Verbs (continued from page 58)

Active voice	In our city, some people are polluting the air.
Effective use of passive voice	In our city, the air **is being polluted**.

Using the Passive Voice Effectively 6–10. Decide whether the active or passive voice is appropriate in each sentence. Revise five sentences that would be more effective in the active voice.

Revising — e-mail

Improvements must be made by our computer club to motivate members. The club's rules were written 15 years ago. Times have changed. Today state-of-the-art equipment is needed by our club. Total membership has been cut in half because there is a lack of adequate facilities.

New computers should be donated by businesses to encourage people to join. Larger meeting rooms should be offered by companies after hours so people can use the equipment.

6. _____
_____

7. _____
_____

8. _____
_____

9. _____
_____

10. _____
_____

Grade 7: Unit 3   Verbs   *(Use with pupil book pages 142–143.)*
Skill: Students will decide when to use the passive voice effectively.

WORKBOOK PLUS 59

13 Subject-Verb Agreement

Singular subjects	The orchestra **rehearses** after school. It **rehearses** daily.
Plural subjects	Most members of the orchestra **play** well. They **play** several instruments.
Compound subjects	Carol and Josh **practice** daily. Neither the flutes nor the recorder **sounds** right. Neither the oboe nor the clarinets **sound** right.

A Write the correct form of the verb in parentheses to complete each sentence.

1. Orchestras or bands (include, includes) a variety of instruments. _____

2. Today many woodwinds (does, do) not have wooden parts. _____

3. The flute (is, are) made of metal. _____

4. The wooden recorder (is, are) a type of flute. _____

5. However, neither its mouthpiece nor its finger holes (resemble, resembles) those of the metal flute. _____

6. Most clarinets (is, are) made of wood. _____

B 7–10. This camp catalogue has four verbs that don't agree with their subjects. Use proofreading marks to correct the catalogue.

Example: Maureen, a flute player in our school band, rehearse^s in the afternoon.

Proofreading Marks
- ¶ Indent
- ∧ Add
- ⌐ Delete
- ≡ Capital letter
- / Small letter
- ⌄⌄ Add quotes
- ∧ Add comma
- ⊙ Add period
- ∩ Transpose

Proofreading

Highlands Music Camp offers many useful courses.

Individual lessons and free-time activities is available.

Neither the pianists nor the voice students attends the orchestra rehearsals.

However, every camper have the option to play in the swing band. Each musician, whether beginner or experienced, enjoy the learning environment at Highlands.

(continued)

Grammar/Usage

Name _____

13 Subject-Verb Agreement (continued from page 60)

Challenge

You are a famous music critic whose opinions on musical matters are highly valued. You have been asked to write a series of articles on music and instruments for your local newspaper. You have decided to begin by writing notes about your opinions and ideas on a variety of musical topics. Do this by adding a predicate to each of the following subjects. Make sure that each subject and verb agree in number.

1. My favorite music _____

2. My favorite musicians _____

3. Either a tuba or a bassoon _____

4. Neither my favorite singer nor my favorite musicians _____

5. Either songwriters or singers _____

6. The opera and the ballet _____

7. Neither drums nor a tambourine _____

8. Marching bands _____

Writing Application: A Newspaper Article — INFORMING

Write a newspaper article about your school orchestra, band, or choral group. Include compound subjects in your article. Make sure that the subjects and verbs in your sentences agree in number.

Grade 7: Unit 3   Verbs   (Use with pupil book pages 144–146.)
Skill: Students will use verbs that agree with singular, plural, and compound subjects.

14 Inverted and Interrupted Order

Inverted order	There **is** an unusual <u>museum</u> in San Francisco. Inside this building **are** many fun <u>exhibits</u>. **Is** the <u>museum</u> called the Exploratorium?
Interrupted order	<u>Visitors</u> to the museum **touch** all the exhibits.

A Write the simple subject of each sentence. Then write the verb in parentheses that agrees with it.

1. There (is, are) many exciting exhibits at the Exploratorium in San Francisco. _____

2. (Does, Do) the teenage guides answer visitors' questions? _____

3. One exhibit on prisms (teach, teaches) us about light. _____

4. A complete visit of the exhibits (take, takes) a few hours. _____

5. In Philadelphia there (is, are) a museum called the Franklin Institute. _____

6. The founders of this museum (was, were) interested in practical demonstrations. _____

B 7–12. This tourist brochure has six verbs that don't agree with their subjects. Use proofreading marks to correct the brochure.

Example: There ~~is~~ ^are^ many attractions in New Orleans.

Proofreading Marks
- ¶ Indent
- ∧ Add
- ℘ Delete
- ≡ Capital letter
- / Small letter
- ❛❜ Add quotes
- ∧ Add comma
- ⊙ Add period
- ∽ Transpose

Proofreading

What is some places to take kids in New Orleans? Here is two museums they're sure to enjoy. Inside the Louisiana Children's Museum are many great things to do. Kids at the Shadow Trap exhibit strikes a pose and then walks away to see their shadow. There are another interesting museum called the Musee Conti Wax Museum. At this famous tourist attraction is life-size wax figures in authentic costumes.

(continued)

Grammar/Usage

Name _____

14 Inverted and Interrupted Order *(continued from page 62)*

Challenge

You work in the information booth at the Museum of Natural History. Many visitors come to you for information. You must be prepared to answer questions about the museum and to direct visitors to various exhibits. Use the museum directory to write the answer to the first question. Then write questions and answers for numbers two through five. Each sentence must be in inverted or interrupted order. The word in parentheses tells you which type of sentence to write.

MUSEUM DIRECTORY

First Floor:	Information (Tours at 1:00 P.M.)
	Gift Shop, Cafeteria
Second Floor:	African, Asian, and North American Mammals
Third Floor:	Insects, Birds, Planetarium
Fourth Floor:	Fish, Amphibians, Reptiles

1. **Question:** Where is the reptile exhibit? _____

   Answer *(inverted)*: _____

2. **Question:** _____

   Answer *(inverted)*: _____

3. **Question:** _____

   Answer *(interrupted)*: _____

4. **Question:** _____

   Answer *(inverted)*: _____

5. **Question:** _____

   Answer *(interrupted)*: _____

Writing Application: A Paragraph

Suppose that you are a tour guide in a museum. You are leading a group of tourists through a new exhibit. Write a paragraph describing the exhibit and the reactions of the tourists. Each sentence should be in inverted or interrupted order.

Grade 7: Unit 3 Verbs *(Use with pupil book pages 147–149.)*
Skill: Students will write sentences in inverted and interrupted order.

Grammar/Usage

Name _____

15 rise, raise; lie, lay; sit, set

Verb	Present Participle	Past	Past Participle	Meaning
rise	(is) rising	rose	(has) risen	to get up, go up
raise	(is) raising	raised	(has) raised	to lift, increase, help to grow
lie	(is) lying	lay	(has) lain	to rest, recline
lay	(is) laying	laid	(has) laid	to put something down, place
sit	(is) sitting	sat	(has) sat	to be seated
set	(is) setting	set	(has) set	to place or put

A Write the correct verb in parentheses to complete each sentence.

1. Our class has (risen, raised) a large amount of money. _____
2. The cost of class trips has (risen, raised). _____
3. Three students were (sitting, setting) behind a table at the craft sale. _____
4. Sandra (lay, laid) some hand-sewn napkins on the table. _____
5. "(Lie, Lay) them by the tablecloths," Hal said. _____
6. Pearl (sat, set) price tags on some pottery. _____
7. By 4:00, only ten items were still (lying, laying) on the tables. _____

B 8–12. This article in a neighborhood newspaper uses five incorrect verbs. Use proofreading marks to correct it.

Example: We laid a mat on the grass and ~~set~~ sat down to eat.

Proofreading Marks
- ¶ Indent
- ∧ Add
- ⸹ Delete
- ≡ Capital letter
- / Small letter
- ⱽⱽ Add quotes
- ⌃ Add comma
- ⊙ Add period
- ∾ Transpose

Proofreading

Elm Street Neighbors Set Goal for New Park

On Saturday the residents of Elm Street had a meeting about rising money for the new park. Some people wanted a lawn where they could lay down and relax. "I like lying my newspaper out on the grass to read," Mrs. Lopez said. Others wanted to raise early each morning and work in a garden. Finally they sit a goal of raising $5,000.

(continued)

WORKBOOK PLUS

Grade 7: Unit 3 Verbs *(Use with pupil book pages 150–152.)*
Skill: Students will use *rise, raise, lie, lay, sit,* and *set* correctly.

Grammar/Usage

Name _____

15 *rise, raise; lie, lay; sit, set* (continued from page 64)

Challenge

You and your aunt are visiting a foreign country. You have risen early in the morning so that you can gaze out your window at the busy marketplace pictured below. Write a page in your travel diary, describing this unusual scene. Use the verbs *rise, raise, lie, lay, sit,* and *set* in your diary page.

_____
_____
_____
_____
_____
_____
_____
_____

Writing Application: A Paragraph

Suppose that you and your family held a garage sale last week. Write a paragraph, describing some of the items that you sold and what your job was at the sale. Use as many verbs from this lesson as possible in your paragraph.

Grade 7: Unit 3 Verbs (Use with pupil book pages 150–152.)
Skill: Students will use *rise, raise, lie, lay, sit,* and *set* correctly.

Grammar/Usage

16 bring, take; let, leave; lend, loan

Word	Present Participle	Past	Past Participle	Meaning
bring	(is) bringing	brought	(has) brought	to carry toward the speaker
take	(is) taking	took	(has) taken	to carry away from the speaker
let	(is) letting	let	(has) let	to allow, permit
leave	(is) leaving	left	(has) left	to go away from, allow to remain
lend	(is) lending	lent	(has) lent	to give something temporarily
loan				something that is lent

A Write the correct word in parentheses to complete each sentence.

1. Hana said that most libraries (lend, loan) more than books. _____

2. She (brought, took) me tapes from the library. _____

3. Some libraries (let, leave) people take out films. _____

4. Last week Hana (loaned, lent) me her favorite book. _____

5. I am (bringing, taking) it back to her tonight. _____

B 6–10. This e-mail message has five incorrect verbs. Use proofreading marks to correct the message.

Example: Do your grandparents ~~leave~~ ^let^ you watch TV?

Proofreading Marks
- ¶ Indent
- ∧ Add
- ꝯ Delete
- ≡ Capital letter
- / Small letter
- ⌄⌄ Add quotes
- ⌃ Add comma
- ⊙ Add period
- ∽ Transpose

e-mail

Would you lend me some CDs for my party? My parents will leave me set up the stereo in the back yard. Maria is taking some new music, and Jack has loan me all of his salsa tapes. Beth leave on vacation yesterday. But she made me a nice lend—a dance light!

(continued)

Grade 7: Unit 3 Verbs *(Use with pupil book pages 153–155.)*
Skill: Students will use *bring, take, let, leave, lend,* and *loan* correctly.

Grammar/Usage

Name _____

16 bring, take; let, leave; lend, loan (continued from page 66)

Challenge

You are tracking the whereabouts of a dangerous double agent. You think that she may be in Montana, but you are not sure. To find out, look back at your notes. First, underline the correct word in each sentence. Then answer each question by writing the clue that goes with each underlined word.

1. What did the agent (bring, take) to me? _____
2. How much was the (lend, loan) that I gave her? _____
3. Did I (let, leave) her use my briefcase? _____
4. Did she (let, leave) New York before 4:00 P.M. Friday? _____
5. What else did I (lend, loan) her? _____
6. Did she (bring, take) it with her? _____

UNDERLINED WORDS	CLUES	UNDERLINED WORDS	CLUES
loan	$1000	bring	secret information
take	yes	leave	no
let	yes	lend	a red sweater

You have just received the additional information below from your special agent in Montana.

> A woman wearing a red sweater and carrying a briefcase was seen in Montana. She was spotted at 5:00 P.M. on Friday.

Could the woman spotted in Montana be the double agent that you are looking for? Use your notes and the additional information to explain why or why not.

_____
_____
_____

Writing Application: Sentences

Suppose that your best friend is going on a trip. You offer this friend the use of your bicycle. Write at least eight sentences that contain tips for your friend. These tips might be about caring for bicycles or bicycle safety. Use as many words from this lesson as possible in your sentences.

Grade 7: Unit 3 Verbs (Use with pupil book pages 153–155.)
Skill: Students will use bring, take, let, leave, lend, and loan correctly.

Revising Strategies: Vocabulary

Name _____

Choosing Different Verbs

          staring   seemed
After ~~looking~~ into the opened box, Dora ~~looked~~ surprised.

1–10. Replace each underlined verb or verb phrase with a word from the word box that has a similar meaning. Be sure the verb you choose fits the meaning of the sentence.

tell	eating	washed	stopped	seemed
watching	expected	considered	appeared	hurried
staring	walked	search	wondered	examined
played	glanced	helping	ran	gazed

Revising

    Darcy was by the window <u>looking</u> for her grandmother to return. While she waited, she decided to <u>look</u> around grandma's attic. Soon Darcy found herself <u>looking</u> at an elaborately engraved silver mechanical pencil. She <u>looked</u> at it closely and found it was filled with lead. The next day she took the pencil to school. Her classmates were impressed with how antique it <u>looked</u>. Darcy decided to use the pencil to answer the multiple-choice questions on her science test. She was a straight A student and <u>looked for</u> the test to be very easy.

    At first it <u>looked</u> as though Darcy knew all the answers. Then she quickly <u>looked</u> at question 6. She was pretty sure that the answer was D. Yet, when she tried to fill in that answer, the pencil would not leave a mark. Nor would it mark the letter A or B. Puzzled, Darcy <u>looked over</u> the answers again. She gave in and marked the letter C. As she left the room, she dropped the silver pencil into the wastebasket. The next day Darcy learned that she was the only one who had scored 100 on the test. The entire class <u>looked</u> at Darcy.

68   **WORKBOOK PLUS**   Grade 7: Unit 3 Verbs (Use with pupil book pages 156–157.)
                               Skill: Students will replace repeated verbs with verbs that have similar meanings.

Grammar

1 Adjectives

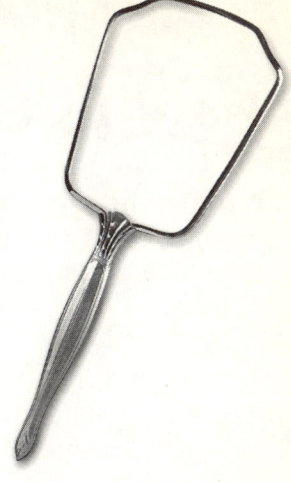

People used **polished metal** surfaces for mirrors in **the colonial** days.
Glass mirrors became **common** in **the** 1700s.
However, they weren't as **sophisticated** as **modern** mirrors.

Write each adjective, including articles. Then write the noun or the pronoun that it modifies.

1. In ancient times people rarely saw good, clear images of themselves.

2. Dim reflections in still water were their mirrors.

3. In the fifth century, the ancient Chinese used bronzed mirrors.

4. This polished metal gave a bright and sharp reflection.

5. Some modern glass mirrors have a thin backing of high-quality silver.

6. Mirrors have many different uses.

7. They can be large or small.

8. A reflecting telescope uses a curved mirror instead of a lens.

(continued)

Grammar

1 Adjectives (continued from page 69)

Challenge

A mirror image is a view shown in reverse. First, decode each riddle below by holding it up to a mirror. Then solve the riddle. Each answer is made up of one adjective and one noun that rhyme.

RIDDLES	DECODED RIDDLES	ANSWERS
happy dog	happy dog	jolly collie
1. colorful boat	1.	
2. large dinosaur bone	2.	
3. noisy group	3.	
4. little stable	4.	
5. fat tree trunk	5.	
6. great rubber band	6.	
7. unusual stove	7.	
8. rugged swamp	8.	
9. big wall	9.	
10. weak bird	10.	
11. large ocean	11.	
12. calm animals	12.	

Writing Application: A Paragraph — EXPRESSING

Suppose you live in a place that has no mirrors. A traveler from another land shows you a mirror. Write a paragraph that describes what you see when you look at yourself for the first time. Use at least two adjectives in each sentence. Underline each adjective.

Revising Strategies: Sentence Fluency

Name _____

Writing with Adjectives

Short sentences	The aardvark is an animal. The aardvark is strange, yet interesting.
Combined sentence	The aardvark is a **strange, yet interesting** animal.

Combining Sentences 1–5. Revise the description. Move adjectives to combine each pair of underlined sentences.

Revising

The aardvark has the common name of earth pig. This is an unfortunate label. Even so, the aardvark is not a pretty sight. This animal resembles a football with a snout, a tail, and four legs. Its legs are short and stubby. Found primarily in Africa and parts of Egypt, the aardvark uses its claws to break open the nests of termites and ants. Then it protrudes its tongue into the nest and captures the insects. Its tongue is sticky.
The aardvark is a timid animal. The aardvark will still defend itself. It butts at an enemy with its shoulders. It swipes at an enemy with its claws and tail. Its claws are sharp and its tail is powerful. Aardvarks can grow to be about 8 feet long from tail to snout.

1. _____

2. _____

3. _____

4. _____

5. _____

(continued)

Grade 7: Unit 4 Modifiers *(Use with pupil book pages 184–185.)*
Skill: Students will combine sentences by moving adjectives.

Revising Strategies: Sentence Fluency

Name _____

Writing with Adjectives (continued from page 71)

Sentence	The tired child fell asleep on the soft, plush armchair.
Transformed sentences	Tired, the child fell asleep on the armchair—soft and plush.
	The child was tired when he fell asleep on the soft, plush armchair.
	The child, tired, fell asleep on an armchair that was soft and plush.

Transforming Sentences 6–10. Revise the underlined sentences by moving adjectives to make the writing more varied and interesting.

Revising

The decorator had to furnish the large study in a mansion that was old and secluded. The study had to be fully redecorated. The decorator was impressed by the massive room and therefore chose elaborate wooden furniture for the desk and chairs. Before bringing in the furniture, she decided to have the walls papered and the floors carpeted. For carpeting she selected a rug that was elegant and handmade.

Looking at the rug design, the decorator could see vines that were winding and leaves shaded in dark green. The wallpaper would have to match the rug at least in theme. She chose a pattern that was pale green with thin, vinelike trim around the border.

6. _____

7. _____

8. _____

9. _____

10. _____

Usage

2 Comparing with Adjectives

Positive Degree	Comparative Degree	Superlative Degree
icy	icier	iciest
careful	more careful	most careful
bad	worse	worst

A Write the correct form of the adjective in parentheses to complete each sentence.

1. The _____ space journey a human has ever made was to the moon. **(longer, longest)**

2. Unpiloted space probes have landed on the planets _____ to Earth. **(most close, closest)**

3. Other probes have gone still _____ distances. **(greater, greatest)**

4. However, none have gone much farther than Pluto, the _____ planet in our system. **(distantest, most distant)**

5. The reason is that even the _____ of all spacecraft is really fairly slow. **(faster, fastest)**

B 6–10. This part of a magazine article has five incorrect adjectives. Use proofreading marks to correct the article.

Example: Earth's moon is ~~largest~~ ^larger^ than the planet Pluto.

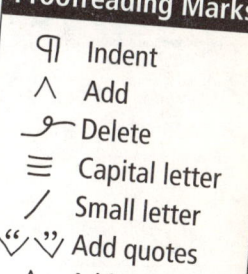

Proofreading Marks
- ¶ Indent
- ∧ Add
- ⌒ Delete
- ≡ Capital letter
- / Small letter
- ⌄⌄ Add quotes
- ⋏ Add comma
- ⊙ Add period
- ∾ Transpose

Take Me to the Moon!

Neil Armstrong, an earliest American astronaut, was the first person to step on our most near neighbor, the moon. He saw mountains more tall than Mt. Everest and craters big than seas. Armstrong and later astronauts returned to earth with the wonderfullest souvenirs—old moon rocks!

(continued)

Grade 7: Unit 4 Modifiers (Use with pupil book pages 186–189.)
Skill: Students will use the comparative and the superlative forms of adjectives.

Usage

Name _____

2 Comparing with Adjectives (continued from page 73)

Challenge

Someday humans may establish colonies on Mars. Suppose that you were raised in a Martian colony. You have just come to Earth as an exchange student, and now you must transmit a report back to Mars. Complete your report below by filling in each blank with a comparative or a superlative adjective.

e-mail

The _____ thing to get used to here is the strong gravity. I am three times _____ here than on Mars. The _____ thing of all is that no one else seems to mind the heaviness!

Except for weighing so much, everything seems _____ here than on Mars. I don't even have to wear a space suit when I go outside!

One of the _____ sights is Earth's moon. It is much _____ than our two tiny Martian moons. The sun is _____ too. That is because Earth is much _____ to the sun than Mars is.

Now add four sentences of your own to the message. Use comparative and superlative adjectives.

_____
_____
_____
_____

Writing Application: A Message

Suppose that you are a space traveler from Earth. You have explored the three recently discovered planets of Syrnx, Akjir, and Ooron. Write a message to send to Earth, comparing the terrain of these three planets. Use comparative and superlative adjectives in your message.

74 WORKBOOK PLUS Grade 7: Unit 4 Modifiers *(Use with pupil book pages 186–189.)*
Skill: Students will use the comparative and the superlative forms of adjectives.

3 Adverbs

When	**Yesterday** we studied the sense of smell.
To what extent	Smells are caused by **very** tiny particles in the air.
How	These particles can move **rapidly**.
Where	They can spread **everywhere**.

Write each adverb. Then write the word or words that it modifies.

1. Bloodhounds can usually track faint scents almost anywhere.

2. Bloodhounds can smell quite keenly.

3. Other animals have really strong senses of smell.

4. Insects often use their extremely sharp sense of smell for communication.

5. The sense of smell is considerably less keen in humans.

6. Sometimes smell alerts us quickly to danger.

7. Have you ever smelled a fire somewhere?

8. The sense of smell is very closely related to the sense of taste.

9. Smell strongly affects our sense of taste.

10. An apple and a raw potato would probably taste the same without your sense of smell.

(continued)

Grade 7: Unit 4 Modifiers *(Use with pupil book pages 190–192.)*
Skill: Students will identify adverbs and the words that they modify.

Grammar

3 Adverbs (continued from page 75)

Challenge

Mel Nice is a cosmetics buyer for a department store. Today he is ordering perfume at a sales show in New York. Help Mel write his report by completing the sentences with adverbs from the perfume bottles below.

exotically
immediately
mysteriously
particularly
very

nearby
easily
secretly
somewhat
newly

regularly
slightly
gladly
soon
there

rather
carefully
extremely
away

really
far
here

    I plan to order several _____ developed perfumes. All the major cosmetics companies _____ display their perfumes _____, so I should _____ find what I want. Because the perfume is _____ expensive, many guards are _____ .

    The first seller I saw _____ _____ opened each bottle for me. One perfume, April Day, smelled _____ delightful. Another perfume, Hawaiian Nights, transported me _____ _____ to _____ strange lands.

    A second salesperson _____ _____ called me to her small booth. _____ she _____ showed me her company's newest fragrance, Millionaire. It _____ did smell like money, _____ moldy and _____ greasy! _____ I decided against buying this perfume. I will _____ inspect more perfumes and make my decision _____ .

Writing Application: A Paragraph — DESCRIBING

    Think of three different scents that you especially like. Suppose you encounter all three smells during a walk. Write a paragraph, describing your walk. Use at least six adverbs in your paragraph. Underline each one.

Writing with Adverbs

Short sentences	The teacher had high expectations for the class. The expectations were justifiable.
Combined sentence	The teacher had **justifiably** high expectations for the class.

Combining Sentences 1–6. Revise the description. Use adverbs to combine the underlined pairs of sentences.

Revising

We walked to the nearest fast food restaurant. We moved in a quick manner. My brother had seen the latest commercial for the child's meal prize. He wanted to get to the restaurant in time. He was frantic. He was certain that the restaurant would run out of Planet X cards before he got there.

We arrived at the restaurant to discover a line more than a block long. We got there soon. Everyone in town seemed to be there. My brother was disappointed. His disappointment was immense. Of course we decided to wait. It was still possible for us to get a prize. The line moved. The movement was slow, but we never wavered. It was finally our turn. My brother ordered his meal and received the last pack of Planet X cards. That was fortunate.

1. _____
2. _____
3. _____
4. _____
5. _____
6. _____

(continued)

Grade 7: Unit 4 Modifiers (Use with pupil book pages 193–194.)
Skill: Students will combine sentences by using adverbs.

Revising Strategies: Sentence Fluency

Name _____

Writing with Adverbs *(continued from page 77)*

Sentence	The guard dog growled at the intruder.
Elaborated sentence	The guard dog growled **ferociously** at the intruder.

Elaborating Sentences 7–14. Revise the description. Use an adverb to modify each underlined word.

Revising

He <u>hit</u> the back door, huffing and puffing. He <u>slammed</u> it behind him. What was that shadowy silhouette <u>twisting</u> in the corner of the yard? As he struggled to catch his breath, he <u>turned</u> to the window that looked out onto the yard. His hot breath <u>condensed</u> on the window, and he could see nothing through the mist. Perhaps it was <u>good</u> that he could not see out. After all, if something <u>was</u> there, what would he do? Suddenly, a door opened. Mike's entire body froze. He heard a rustling and the scuffle of feet. "Well, son, how was your <u>first</u> time home alone?"

Grade 7: Unit 4 Modifiers *(Use with pupil book pages 193–194.)*
Skill: Students will use adverbs to add details and elaborate sentences.

4 Comparing with Adverbs

Positive degree	early	rapidly	often	well
Comparative degree	earlier	more rapidly	less often	better
Superlative degree	earliest	most rapidly	least often	best

A Write the comparative or superlative form of the adverb in parentheses.

1. Successes and failures generally occur _____ in sports than in other activities. **(frequently)**

2. Of all players, the losers blame the officials _____ . **(often)**

3. Do the losers criticize themselves _____ than the winners do? **(harshly)**

4. Would the outcome of the game have been different if someone had reached a few inches _____ during a specific play? **(far)**

5. A good player usually realizes that the other team simply played _____ . **(well)**

B 6–10. This part of a sports guide has five incorrect adverbs. Use proofreading marks to correct the guide.

Example: The top college scorers are usually chosen most quick by pro teams. (with "ly" inserted after "quick")

Proofreading Marks
- ¶ Indent
- ∧ Add
- ↪ Delete
- ≡ Capital letter
- / Small letter
- ⌄⌄ Add quotes
- ∧ Add comma
- ⊙ Add period
- ∿ Transpose

Proofreading

Women began playing basketball latest than men.

Women's basketball most finally became an Olympic event in 1976, and in 1982 Louisiana Tech happily won the NCAA's first women's college championship. But professional leagues appeared more recent. Two leagues formed in the 1990s. Some fans said the American Basketball League played more well than the Women's National Basketball Association, but the WNBA marketed its teams successful.

(continued)

Grade 7: Unit 4 Modifiers *(Use with pupil book pages 195–197.)*
Skill: Students will use the comparative and the superlative forms of adverbs.

Grammar/Usage

4 Comparing with Adverbs (continued from page 79)

Challenge

Guido, Kita, Larry, and Lina pitch for the Watson Little League baseball team. Below are their records for the 2000 season.

	Guido	Kita	Larry	Lina
GAMES PLAYED	10	8	12	15
WON	4	6	7	8
LOST	6	2	5	7
TIMES AT BAT	27	21	24	31
HOME RUNS	1	5	3	4

Compare the records of the four pitchers. Fill in the blanks with comparative and superlative adverbs.

1. Of all the pitchers, Lina played _____.

2. Larry pitched _____ than Guido.

3. Of all the players, Kita batted _____ often.

4. Lina won _____ than Guido.

5. Of all the players, Kita lost _____.

6. Lina hit home runs _____ than Larry.

Now write two sentences of your own, using the chart above. Include a comparative or superlative adverb in each sentence.

7. _____

8. _____

Writing Application: Creative Writing

If you could be best in the world at just one thing, what would it be? Write a paragraph, telling about your choice and why you made it. Use at least two comparative and two superlative adverbs in your sentences.

Grade 7: Unit 4 Modifiers (Use with pupil book pages 195–197.)
Skill: Students will use comparative and superlative adverbs.

Grammar/Usage

Name _____

5 Negatives

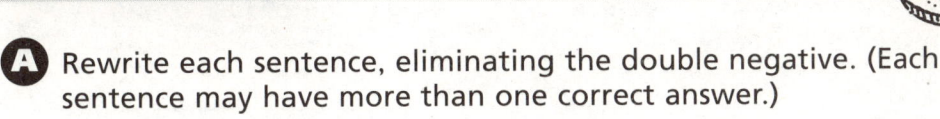

Double negative	**Don't** take **no** wooden nickels.
Correct	**Don't** take any wooden nickels.
Correct	Take **no** wooden nickels.

A Rewrite each sentence, eliminating the double negative. (Each sentence may have more than one correct answer.)

1. "You're not never too old to learn."
   _____

2. "All that glitters is not scarcely gold."
   _____

3. Haven't you never heard these old sayings?
   _____

4. The first one is so old that not no one knows where it came from.
   _____

5. The second is from Shakespeare, but you won't find it in none of his plays.
   _____

B 6–8. This part of a tourist brochure has two double negatives. Use proofreading marks to correct the sentences.

Example: In Pennsylvania the fun doesn't ~~never~~ stop until the cows come home.

Proofreading Marks
- ¶ Indent
- ∧ Add
- ⌐ Delete
- ≡ Capital letter
- / Small letter
- ⌄⌄ Add quotes
- ⋀ Add comma
- ⊙ Add period
- ∽ Transpose

Proofreading

Don't miss seeing the countryside of Pennsylvania.

Another place you wouldn't hardly want to skip is Gettysburg, in Adams County.

History students won't never forget this important Civil War battle site.

(continued)

Grade 7: Unit 4 Modifiers *(Use with pupil book pages 198–200.)*
Skill: Students will correct double negatives.

WORKBOOK PLUS **81**

Grammar/Usage

5 Negatives (continued from page 81)

Challenge

Bea Wyse is a very smart person. People travel hundreds of miles to hear her words of wisdom. However, she has difficulty wording some of her sayings. Write each wise saying correctly.

1. Don't never cry over spilled milk.
2. A rolling stone scarcely gathers no moss.
3. You can't hardly judge a book by its cover.
4. Time never waits for no one.
5. Never leave no stone unturned.
6. People who live in glass houses shouldn't throw no stones.

1. _____
2. _____
3. _____
4. _____
5. _____
6. _____

Now write the number of each saying you wrote beside its meaning.

_____ Appearances are deceiving.   _____ It's good to keep moving.

_____ Don't miss an opportunity.   _____ What's done is done.

_____ Try every option.   _____ Don't criticize others.

Writing Application: Proverbs — CREATING

"A shoe may walk many miles, yet never become a foot." Some people might think that this proverb is a wise saying. Others might think that it's just silly. Write four proverbs of your own. Make them silly or serious. Be sure to avoid double negatives.

82 WORKBOOK PLUS

Grade 7: Unit 4   Modifiers   (Use with pupil book pages 198–200.)
Skill: Students will use negatives correctly.

Grammar/Usage

Name _____

6 Adjective or Adverb?

Adjectives	Adverbs
Some commercials are **good**.	Writers write them **well**.
The actors act like **real** people.	They make them **really** believable.
The actors don't feel **well** today.	They can't perform **badly**.

Write the correct word in parentheses to complete each sentence.

1. A lot of TV commercials are (certain, certainly) dull. _____

2. However, a commercial done (good, well) is fun to watch. _____

3. An excellent commercial is (amazing, amazingly) difficult to make. _____

4. The situation shown in the commercial must be (believable, believably). _____

5. The actors must look (comfortable, comfortably) as they work. _____

6. The camera must capture everything (clear, clearly). _____

7. The director must tie everything (neat, neatly) together. _____

8. The effect of a good commercial on the viewer can be very (strong, strongly). _____

9. This is quite (surprising, surprisingly) when you remember that the average commercial is only thirty seconds long. _____

10. Imagine developing an interesting story and likable characters in such a (short, shortly) time. _____

11. Some actors feel that commercial work is not (real, really) as difficult as acting in plays. _____

12. Most actors, though, like making commercials, and many agree that the salary is (good, well)! _____

(continued)

Grade 7: Unit 4 Modifiers (Use with pupil book pages 201–203.)
Skill: Students will distinguish between adverbs and adjectives.

6 Adjective or Adverb? (continued from page 83)

Challenge

You work for an advertising agency. Your job is writing slogans for different products. For each product pictured below, write a slogan to promote the product. Use adjectives and adverbs in the slogans.

SLOGAN: _____

SLOGAN: _____

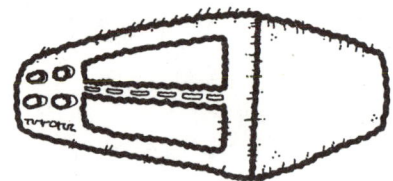

SLOGAN: _____

SLOGAN: _____

Now create two new products. Draw a picture and write a slogan for each one.

SLOGAN: _____

SLOGAN: _____

Writing Application: A Commercial

People who write commercials use many adjectives and adverbs. Write a short commercial about your favorite product. Use the words *good, well, bad,* and *badly* in your commercial.

Revising Strategies: Vocabulary

Name _____

Choosing Different Adjectives and Adverbs

>   considerate   presently
> He is a ~~nice~~ person and will ~~now~~ help us with our work.

1–10. Replace each overused adjective *nice* and overused adverb *now* with a word or phrase from the word box that has a similar meaning. Be sure the expression you choose fits the meaning of the sentence.

caring	immediately	instantly	right away
later	before	while	in the evening
considerate	likable	thoughtful	happily
strange	presently	at this time	kind
wasteful	surprising	wrong	angry

Revising

    Mr. Henry was always considered a <u>nice</u> teacher. He was very <u>nice</u> about letting students make up tests. He always gave them time to do their work—unlike Mr. Finley, who always expected his students to finish their work <u>now</u>. So <u>now</u> it came as a big surprise to Mr. Henry's students when he told them to hand in their book reports <u>now</u>. The reports were due tomorrow. This was not very <u>nice</u> of Mr. Henry. Nor was it typical. It was something the students expected from Mr. Finley, who was not as <u>nice</u>.

    As it happened, most of the students did not <u>now</u> have their reports with them. They explained this to Mr. Henry, who opened his marking book. "Then I will give you all zeros <u>now</u>," he said. When he read his book, he realized he had made a mistake. He said, "I see your reports are due tomorrow and not today. I will be <u>nice</u> and let you hand them in next week instead."

Grade 7: Unit 4 Modifiers (Use with pupil book page 204.)
Skill: Students will replace repeated adjectives and adverbs with adjectives and adverbs that have similar meanings.

Mechanics

Name _____

1 Correct Sentences

Declarative	Many sailors roamed the seas before Columbus.
Interrogative	Did any of them reach the Americas?
Exclamatory	What dangerous feats they performed!
Imperative	Read about these early voyages.

A Label each sentence *declarative, interrogative, exclamatory,* or *imperative*. Then rewrite each sentence, using correct capitalization and end punctuation.

1. have you ever heard of Eric the Red _____

2. he founded the first settlement in Greenland _____

3. what tremendous courage and skill he had _____

4. trace his journey on a map _____

B 5–10. This part of a biography has six sentences with punctuation errors. Use proofreading marks to correct the sentences.

Example: Have you ever heard of Robert E. Peary.

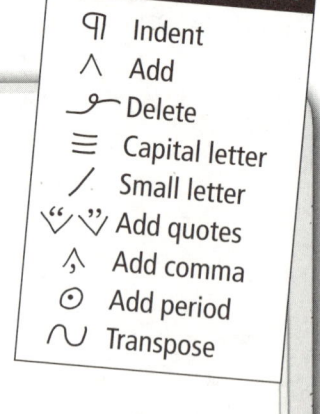

Proofreading Marks
¶ Indent
∧ Add
⌒ Delete
≡ Capital letter
/ Small letter
⌄⌄ Add quotes
∧ Add comma
⊙ Add period
∪ Transpose

Proofreading

In the 1880s Robert E. Peary began gathering support to explore the Arctic? Geographers of the day asked important questions about the region? was Greenland part of North America Was the sea under the North Pole shallow.

during his Arctic expeditions, Peary discovered that Greenland was an island and that the Arctic Ocean was deep! what an adventure he had?

(continued)

WORKBOOK PLUS Grade 7: Unit 5 Capitalization and Punctuation *(Use with pupil book pages 222–223.)*
Skill: Students will identify, capitalize, and punctuate the four types of sentences.

Mechanics

Name _____

1 Correct Sentences (continued from page 86)

Challenge

The incomplete sentences below are from a ship's log. Rewrite the sentences by supplying the information that answers the questions in parentheses. Be sure to capitalize and punctuate each sentence correctly.

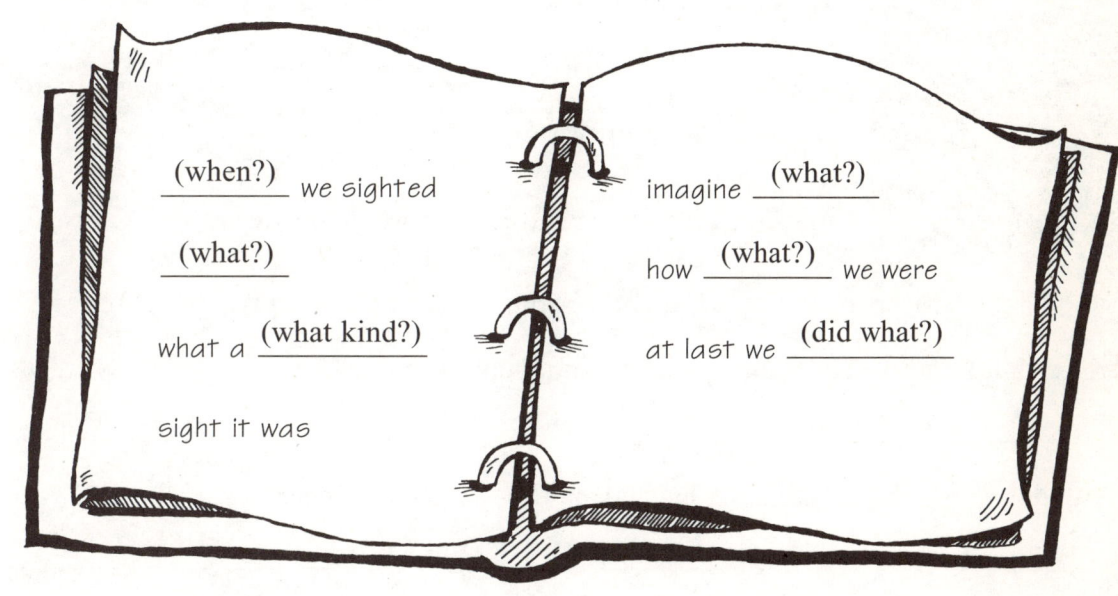

_____
_____
_____
_____
_____

Writing Application: Dialogue

Two explorers meet each other on a deserted island. Each claims to have discovered the island. Write a dialogue that takes place between them. By the end of the dialogue, the two explorers should have come to some kind of agreement. Include each of the four types of sentences at least once. When you are finished, read your dialogue aloud with a partner. Use your voice to show the different types of sentences.

Grade 7: Unit 5 Capitalization and Punctuation (Use with pupil book pages 222–223.)
Skill: Students will identify, capitalize, and punctuate the four types of sentences.

Mechanics

2 Proper Nouns and Proper Adjectives

People	Dr. J. B. Wei, Koreans
Institutions	Yale University
Places	the South, Bay of Fundy
Languages	Chinese, French
Days	Tuesday, Wednesday, Friday
Events	Industrial Revolution
Months	February, July, December
Periods	Ice Age
Organizations	League of Women Voters
Documents	Stamp Act
Proper adjectives	Japanese engineers, January thaw, Atlantic waters

Rewrite each sentence, capitalizing the proper nouns and the proper adjectives.

1. Next fall kimi will attend the university of miami in florida.

2. While touring the white house, lou and aunt di saw the president.

3. My aunt saw greek statues and stone age tools at a british museum.

4. Did president lincoln sign the emancipation proclamation?

5. Please call dr. b. f. washington jr. by friday, may 2.

6. During his trip through the west, dale saw lake mead and zion canyon.

7. The ambassador bridge touches both the united states and canada.

8. Our mayor, mayor li, sent the red cross to the disaster area.

(continued)

Mechanics Name _____

2 Proper Nouns and Proper Adjectives (continued from page 88)

Challenge

Solve each puzzle below by writing a proper noun or a proper adjective and a noun. Each word in your answer must begin with the same first letter as each word in the clue. Be sure to use capital letters correctly.

1. wonderful musician _____
2. sandy area _____
3. noted astronaut _____
4. mighty rivulet _____
5. amazing buffalo _____
6. wonderful tower creation _____
7. European crossing _____
8. *Little Men* author _____
9. statesman, writer, Conservative _____
10. alarming rebellion _____
11. famous nurse _____
12. Cantonese lamp _____
13. Washington home _____
14. pilgrim community _____
15. high mounds _____
16. powerful painter _____

Writing Application: An Invitation — DESCRIBING

Suppose that you are inviting a friend to spend a week with you. You have made plans to visit many interesting people and places in your town or city. Write a letter to your friend, describing your plans for the week. Include five proper nouns and five proper adjectives in your letter.

Grade 7: Unit 5 Capitalization and Punctuation (Use with pupil book pages 224–227.)
Skill: Students will write proper nouns and proper adjectives correctly.

3 Interjections

Common Interjections		
ah	hurray	ouch
aha	oh	ugh
good grief	oh, no	whew
hey	oops	wow

Hey, look at this picture of the planets.
Wow! Which one is that?

Write an interjection and the correct punctuation for each sentence.

1. _____ We are finally at the planetarium!

2. _____ come look through this telescope.

3. _____ I can see the planet Jupiter.

4. _____ It is huge!

5. _____ it says here that Jupiter is the most massive planet.

6. _____ that is the planet Saturn.

7. _____ I bet those rings are made of some kind of gas.

8. _____ They're made of ice particles and rock!

9. _____ Temperatures around the planet get as low as −300°F!

10. _____ I wouldn't want to be anywhere near there!

11. _____ Be careful with that telescope!

12. _____ he almost broke it.

13. _____ This is the best planetarium I've ever visited!

14. _____ That was my toe you stepped on.

15. _____ I never realized that the planet Neptune was such a beautiful deep blue color.

16. _____ did you know that Pluto is the smallest planet?

17. _____ we have to hurry. The planetarium is closing soon.

18. _____ We're locked in!

(continued)

Usage

Name _____

3 Interjections (continued from page 90)

Challenge

Write the dialogue for a story about two people who have just opened the door of their spaceship on another planet. Fill in each box with an interjection and the correct punctuation. Fill in each blank with conversation that goes along with each interjection. Afterward, create a drawing to illustrate the story.

" [ ] _____ !" the captain said.

" [ ] _____ !" the assistant answered, feeling the same excitement.

The two walked a little farther from their craft.

" [ ] _____ ," the captain suddenly exclaimed in alarm.

" [ ] _____ ," the assistant said unhappily.

The captain went to take a closer look.

" [ ] _____ ," the embarrassed leader admitted.

" [ ] _____ ," the assistant replied.

Writing Application: Interview — PERSUADING

You have just returned from a newly discovered planet and will be interviewed on the evening news. Write down the questions you think will be asked and the answers you plan to give. Include a few interjections in the interview.

Mechanics

4 Uses for Commas

Dogs, cats, and other animals need medical care.
Some veterinarians examine, treat, and board animals.
They may work in offices, on farms, or in zoos.
We bought a puppy, and our vet examined it.

Rewrite the sentences, adding commas if they are needed.

1. Veterinarians are doctors but their patients are not humans.

2. Their patients may be cats birds turtles or giraffes.

3. Vets give vaccinations prescribe medicine and perform surgery.

4. Vets may specialize in the care of pets farm animals or zoo animals.

5. Some vets examine only cats and others treat only horses.

6. A tiger an elephant or a monkey may be a vet's patient.

7. A city vet works in an office but a farm vet makes house calls.

8. Vets and their assistants help keep animals healthy.

9. Do you love animals enjoy science and get good grades?

10. Find a job with a vet and this job might become your career.

(continued)

WORKBOOK PLUS   Grade 7: Unit 5 Capitalization and Punctuation (Use with pupil book pages 230–232.)
Skill: Students will use commas in a series and in compound sentences.

Mechanics

Name _____

4 Uses for Commas (continued from page 92)

Challenge

Suppose that you are attending a lecture at the School of Veterinary Medicine. The professor has written some important words and phrases on the board. Arrange these words and phrases into five lists. The words and phrases on each list should be related in some way. Write your lists on a separate piece of paper.

```
test tubes           heart is monitored      in a hospital
learn new            diagnoses               form study groups
  techniques         pulse is taken          slides
examines             microscope              prescribes
in an office         in a kennel
```

Now write five sentences that tell what information you learned at the lecture. Use each list of words to write a compound sentence or a sentence containing a series. Be sure to use commas correctly.

1. _____
2. _____
3. _____
4. _____
5. _____

Writing Application: A Letter

Suppose that you are applying for a job as a veterinarian's helper. Write a letter, explaining why you think that you would be good at this job. Include at least two compound sentences and three sentences containing a series of three or more items. Be sure to use commas correctly.

Grade 7: Unit 5 Capitalization and Punctuation *(Use with pupil book pages 230–232.)*
Skill: Students will use commas in a series and in compound sentences.

Writing Sentences with Commas

Short sentences	As an infant, Helen Keller became ill. She was left deaf and blind. She became mute.
Combined sentence	As an infant, Helen Keller **became ill, was left deaf and blind, and became mute**.

Combining Sentences: Words and Phrases in a Series 1–5. Revise the description. Combine each set of underlined sentences by using words or phrases in a series.

Revising

Anne Sullivan, Helen Keller's teacher, had problems of her own. <u>She had poor vision. She was raised in poverty. She had few friends.</u> By the time Anne was ten years old, her life became even more tragic. <u>She lost her mother to illness. She was abandoned by her father. She was sent to a state hospital for the poor.</u> While at the hospital, Anne showed a great deal of ambition. <u>She eventually went to school. She learned to read with her fingers. She graduated in 1886 with the highest honors in her class.</u>

After graduating, Anne Sullivan was hired to be a private tutor in Tuscumbia, Alabama. She expected to find a shy, quiet student. What a surprise it was to Anne when she met Helen Keller. <u>Helen was a spoiled child. She was demanding. She acted in a stubborn manner.</u> Her parents had given her everything she wanted. Eventually Anne was able to teach Helen to use her hands to communicate. <u>Helen came to love Anne. She began to respect her. She felt gratitude toward Anne.</u>

1. _____

2. _____

3. _____

4. _____

5. _____

(continued)

Revising Strategies: Sentence Fluency

Writing Sentences with Commas (continued from page 94)

Simple sentences	We studied about westward expansion. We made posters about the movement. We displayed them around the room.
Combined sentence	We studied about westward expansion, **we** made posters about the movement, **and we** displayed them around the room.

Combining Sentences: Clauses in a Series 6–10. Combine each set of underlined sentences by placing clauses in a series. Use a conjunction to connect them.

Revising

In the 19th century the United States enjoyed a great westward expansion. Pioneers packed their worldly possessions into wooden wagons. They set out on the Oregon Trail. They traveled westward into the unknown. For them, it was an adventure. The journey took four to six months. It was filled with danger. Travelers often died from disease. The Oregon Trail was little more than a rough path. Pioneers had to float their wagons across rivers. They climbed the Rocky Mountains and the Blue Mountains. They faced the constant threats of starvation and attack.

Today travel time has been cut. Superhighways make the journey smooth. The beauty of the scenery remains. The West still draws millions of visitors. Modern travelers can enjoy the majesty of the mountains. They can witness the orange sunsets. They can watch a herd of deer scamper for cover in the wilderness.

6. _____

7. _____

8. _____

9. _____

10. _____

Grade 7: Unit 5 Capitalization and Punctuation (Use with pupil book pages 233–234.)
Skill: Students will use clauses in a series to combine sentences.

Mechanics

Name _____

5 More Uses for Commas

Introductory words	Toni, have you heard of Ernest Shackleton? Yes, I read a book about his adventures.
Interrupters	Shackleton, a polar explorer, was British. As a matter of fact, he did not reach his goal. He did save all of his crew, however.

A Rewrite the sentences, adding commas where they are needed.

1. Ernest Shackleton a daring hero loved excitement.
   _____

2. He left for Antarctica Toni in the summer of 1914.
   _____

3. He wanted to cross the continent by way of the South Pole I believe.
   _____

4. Well the crew camped on the ice after the ship broke apart.
   _____

B 5–8. This imaginary interview with a historical figure has four missing or incorrect commas. Use proofreading marks to correct the interview.

Example: Annie Smith Peck⌃a mountaineer⌃climbed Peru's Mt. Huascarán in 1908.

Proofreading Marks
- ¶ Indent
- ∧ Add
- ⌐ Delete
- ≡ Capital letter
- / Small letter
- ⌄⌄ Add quotes
- ⌃ Add comma
- ⊙ Add period
- ∿ Transpose

Proofreading

Interviewer:	Ms. Peck where did you first become interested in mountains?
Peck:	While traveling in Switzerland, I fell in love with the Alps.
Interviewer:	Did you climb, Mt. Shasta or the Matterhorn, first?
Peck:	Well I climbed Mt. Shasta before the Matterhorn.

(continued)

Mechanics

Name _____

5 More Uses for Commas (continued from page 96)

Challenge

Read the following conversation between two polar explorers. Write introductory words and interrupters to complete the sentences. Use commas correctly.

Nolina: What are you doing _____ ?

Loni: I'm measuring the depth of the ice _____ .

Nolina: _____ how deep is it?

Loni: It is _____ only a few feet thick. It could break apart tomorrow _____ .

Nolina: We could _____ be here forever!

Now finish the conversation. Use an introductory word or an interrupter in each sentence.

Loni: _____
_____

Nolina: _____
_____

Loni: _____
_____

Nolina: _____
_____

Writing Application: An Interview

Suppose that you interviewed a member of Shackleton's crew. Write the questions that you asked this crew member. Then write the answers that the person gave you. Use different kinds of introductory words and interrupters in your interview. Be sure to use commas correctly.

Grade 7: Unit 5 Capitalization and Punctuation *(Use with pupil book pages 235–237.)*
Skill: Students will use commas to set off introductory words and interrupters.

6 Dates, Addresses, and Letters

Dates and Addresses	Greetings and Closings
October 21, 2002	Dear Aunt Sally,
200 Lincoln Street	Dear Senator Gale:
Richfield, MN 55423	Sincerely yours,

Rewrite the letter, using correct capitalization and punctuation.

> 505 hilldale road
> longview tx 75602
> march 9 2000
>
> dear nancy
>   please come to a surprise party for Kim Lee. it will be held at 34 valley road longview texas on march 24 2000 at two o'clock. let me know by march 15 if you can come.
>
>   your friend
>   stewart ritter

(continued)

Mechanics

6 Dates, Addresses, and Letters *(continued from page 98)*

Challenge

Yule Findit, a detective, is looking for a new job. He answered an ad in the paper with the letter below. Unfortunately he wrote part of the letter in code, and he forgot to use capital letters and punctuation marks. Help Yule get the job. First, decode each boxed clue.

---

421 vine street appleton wi 54911 august 13 2000

weknow detective agency 1227 south street grinnell ia 50112

dear sir or madam [once / a time] , I was an agent who [cover / worked]

since june 1998 [job I've been job] [stand / I] that [noon this] you

are interviewing applicants I will [be / joyed] and [ever ever / ever ever] grateful

if you grant me an interview sincerely yours yule findit

Now, on a separate piece of paper, rewrite the letter, using correct capitalization and punctuation.

Writing Application: A Letter — EXPLAINING

Write a letter inviting a relative to your class play. Include a heading that gives your address and the date. Also include an address and a date that tell where and when the play will be held. Be sure to use correct capitalization and punctuation.

Mechanics

Name _____

7 Direct Quotations

Direct quotations	Why did Ellen say, "Bird watchers love Audubon"? "Audubon was a famous wildlife painter," she said. "Mainly," she added, "he painted birds."
Indirect quotation	Ellen explained that he was one of the first to paint the birds of the United States.

A Rewrite each sentence, using correct capitalization and punctuation.

1. John Audubon explained Ellen taught himself to paint.
   _____

2. He devoted his whole life to painting birds added Carl.
   _____

3. He loved birds said Joy he could think of nothing else.
   _____

4. Was he the greatest wildlife artist in the United States she asked.
   _____

B 5–8. This conversation has four direct quotations with incorrect punctuation and capitalization. Use proofreading marks to correct the conversation.
Example: ⋎John Audubon was born in Haiti,⋏said Randall.

Proofreading Marks
- ¶ Indent
- ∧ Add
- ℒ Delete
- ≡ Capital letter
- / Small letter
- ⋎ ⋏ Add quotes
- ∧ Add comma
- ⊙ Add period
- ∽ Transpose

Proofreading

Randall said, I just read a book about John Audubon

Where did Audubon grow up asked Keisha?

in France answered Randall, according to this book.

Keisha asked, "When did he come to the United States?"

he came in 1803 Replied Randall his father sent him to a farm near

Philadelphia, where he began drawing birds."

(continued)

100 **WORKBOOK PLUS**
▲■

Grade 7: Unit 5 Capitalization and Punctuation (Use with pupil book pages 241–243.)
Skill: Students will capitalize and will punctuate quotations.

Mechanics Name _____

7 Direct Quotations (continued from page 100)

Challenge

A book character named Tom Swift always said things in a special way. Look at these examples of "Tom Swifties."

"Is the glass **transparent**?" Tom asked **clearly**.

"Look at its **long, sharp** beak," I said **pointedly**.

Suppose that you and Tom Swift are friends. One day you both go bird watching. Complete each direct quotation with a word from the box. Then add the correct capitalization and punctuation. Use proofreading marks.

| fruitlessly | soundly | heavily | loudly | repeatedly | crossly |

1. What is that bird squawking at Tom asked _____ .

2. How much do you think this bird weighs? I asked _____ .

3. Did you hear its call Tom questioned _____ .

4. One bird I said _____ has been singing for hours.

5. Tom remarked _____ it didn't eat any of those berries.

6. Don't make any noise said Tom _____ the bird might fly away.

Now, on a separate piece of paper, write four "Tom Swifties" of your own. Be sure that you use correct capitalization and punctuation.

Writing Application: A Dialogue

Imagine that you live in the 1800s and that you want to be John Audubon's assistant. Write a dialogue in which you discuss with Audubon how you became interested in bird watching.

Grade 7: Unit 5 Capitalization and Punctuation (Use with pupil book pages 241–243.)
Skill: Students will write direct quotations correctly.

Mechanics

8 Titles

Books	Jo's Boys	Plays	Cats
TV series	Family Ties	Ships	Merrimac
Magazines	Newsweek	Short stories	"A Day's Wait"
Works of art	Mona Lisa	Articles	"The First Thanksgiving"
Newspapers	USA Today	Poems	"Note to My Neighbor"
Planes	Spirit of St. Louis	Book chapters	"Navajo Home"

Rewrite each sentence, correcting each title.

1. Mother actually saw the first launch of the space shuttle columbia.

2. I finished the chapter up and about in johnny tremain.

3. Vincent van Gogh created the painting starry night.

4. Mrs. Claussen liked the book flowers for algernon.

5. The article a room with a view appeared in the magazine newsweek.

6. Follow me is a song from the musical Camelot.

7. Ed recited the poem kid in the park by Langston Hughes.

8. Today's daily tribune published a review of the movie fantasia.

9. We enjoy watching masterpiece theatre on television.

(continued)

Mechanics

Name _____

8 Titles (continued from page 102)

Challenge

There are eleven titles hidden in the story below. Find the titles and write them on the lines. Add quotation marks and underlining where they are needed.

One day, Susanna set out for a walk down by the old mill stream. On the way she met Johnny Tremain and his new friend. "Oh! Susanna," called Johnny. "I'd like you to meet Annabel Lee. I met Annabel when I visited Oklahoma!"

The three continued down Sesame Street. Annabel added, "This afternoon, if we have enough time, I hope Johnny will take me out to the ball game, so I can see Casey at the bat."

As they walked, they discussed how to play baseball. In the distance they heard what they thought was the sound of music, but it was only the wind in the willows.

1. Song: _ _ _ _ _ _ _ _ _ _ _ _ _ _ _
   _ _ _ _ _ _ _ _ _ _ _

2. Book: _ _ _ _ _ _ _ _ _ _ _ _ _

3. Song: _ _ ! _ _ _ _ _ _ _ _

4. Poem: _ _ _ _ _ _ _ _ _ _

5. Play: _ _ _ _ _ _ _ _ _ _ !

6. TV Series: _ _ _ _ _ _ _ _ _ _ _

7. Magazine: _ _ _

8. Song: _ _ _ _ _ _ _ _ _ _
   _ _ _ _ _ _ _ _

9. Poem: _ _ _ _ _ _ _ _ _ _

10. Movie: _ _ _ _ _ _ _ _ _ _ _

11. Book: _ _ _ _ _ _ _ _ _ _ _
    _ _ _ _ _

Writing Application: A Letter — DESCRIBING

Write a letter to a friend, recommending some things that you have enjoyed reading, listening to, or watching. Include at least six titles. Be sure to use underlining and quotation marks correctly.

Grade 7: Unit 5 Capitalization and Punctuation *(Use with pupil book pages 244–246.)*
Skill: Students will write titles correctly.

Mechanics

Name _____

9 Semicolons and Colons

Semicolons	Yellowstone is magnificent; it has many natural wonders.
Colons	Our train leaves at 8:53 P.M. Wednesday. Dear Ms. Bennett: You will need the following: a backpack, boots, and extra socks.

A Rewrite each sentence, adding a semicolon or a colon where it is needed.

1. Nita took a vacation she went to Yellowstone National Park.

2. There she saw the following animals bison, elk, and bears.

3. Nita rose by 5 30 A.M.

4. She took equipment binoculars, a notebook, and a guidebook.

B 5–8. This post card has four incorrect or missing semicolons and colons. Correct it, using proofreading marks.

Example: To get to the Grand Canyon, we drove through four states; Wyoming, Idaho, Utah, and Arizona.

Proofreading Marks
- ¶ Indent
- ∧ Add
- ꝯ Delete
- ≡ Capital letter
- / Small letter
- ⌄⌄ Add quotes
- ∧ Add comma
- ⊙ Add period
- ∽ Transpose

Proofreading

Dear Mr. Stark,

Yesterday we arrived at the Grand Canyon the sun was just setting. I wish you and Mrs. Stark could have seen the colors red, brown, orange, yellow, and purple. I hope you're doing well say: hello to Mrs. Stark.

Sincerely, Maureen

(continued)

104 **WORKBOOK PLUS**

Grade 7: Unit 5 Capitalization and Punctuation *(Use with pupil book pages 247–249.)*
Skill: Students will use semicolons and colons correctly.

Mechanics

Name _____

9 Semicolons and Colons (continued from page 104)

Challenge

Chita and Rita were taking a trip to Yellowstone National Park. Find out what happened to them at the airport. Rewrite each set of words as a sentence. Use semicolons and colons correctly.

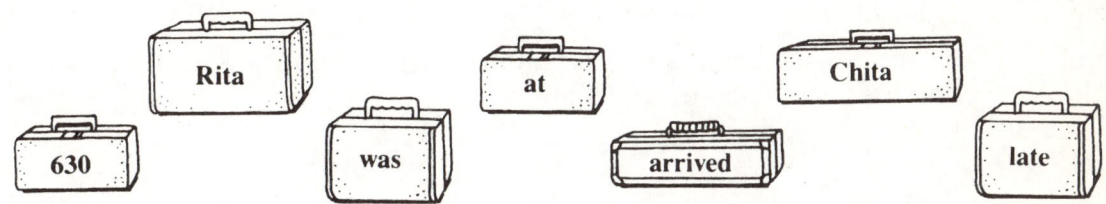

1. _____

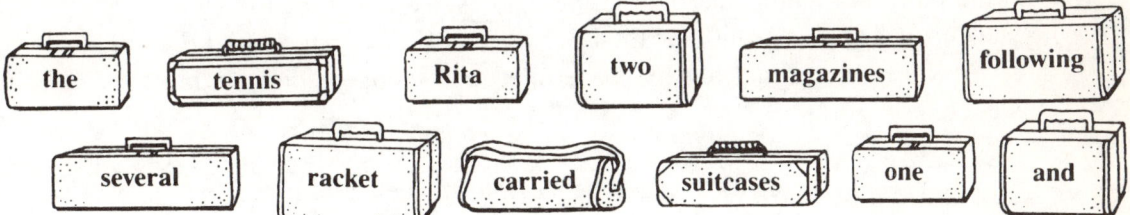

2. _____

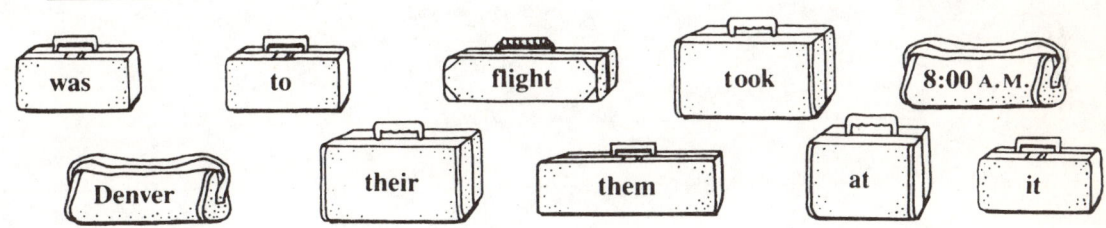

3. _____

On a separate piece of paper, write six sentences, describing the highlights of a trip that you've taken or a trip that you plan to take. Include a colon or a semicolon in each sentence.

Writing Application: A Letter

You are a travel agent. Write a letter to a customer, giving specific information about a tour of a national park. Use at least two semicolons and four colons in your letter.

Grade 7: Unit 5 Capitalization and Punctuation (Use with pupil book pages 247–249.)

Skill: Students will use semicolons and colons correctly.

WORKBOOK PLUS 105

Revising Strategies: Sentence Fluency

Name _____

Writing Sentences with Semicolons and Colons

Short sentences	Scientists have been studying outer space for years. However, there is still so much they do not understand.
Combined sentence	Scientists have been studying outer space for years; **however,** there is still so much they do not understand.

Combining Sentences with Semicolons 1–5. Revise the description. Combine each pair of underlined sentences by using a semicolon.

Revising

We are all familiar with holes. They are part of our everyday existence. We find them in our clothes or aim a ball at them in golf. Few of us are familiar with the holes in outer space. These black holes, as they are called, are truly mysterious. German astronomer Karl Schwarzschild first suggested the concept in 1916. Recent investigations by space telescope seem to confirm their existence.

The term "black hole" sounds sinister. Nevertheless, it is an accurate description. Today's scientists continue to find this celestial phenomenon a source of wonderment. Nothing that enters the horizon of a black hole escapes. Even light and gravity are affected. What about time? Time slows down as it approaches a black hole. Once inside, it ceases to exist.

1. _____
2. _____
3. _____
4. _____
5. _____

(continued)

Grade 7: Unit 5 Capitalization and Punctuation *(Use with pupil book pages 250–251.)*
Skill: Students will combine sentences by using semicolons.

Revising Strategies: Sentence Fluency

Name _____

Writing Sentences with Semicolons and Colons (continued from page 106)

Sentences	We plan to visit several tourist attractions. We will visit the caverns and the alligator exhibit and the bird sanctuary.
Combined sentence	We plan to visit several tourist attractions: **the caverns, the alligator exhibit, and the bird sanctuary.**

Combining Sentences with Colons 6–10. Trim down the description. Combine each set of underlined sentences by using a colon.

Revising

My drive along the coast will take me through several states. The states I will pass through are North Carolina, South Carolina, Georgia, and Florida. Since I will be traveling for several weeks, I will need clothes for both warm and cold weather. I plan to pack different types of clothing. The clothes will include sweaters, shirts, shorts, and pants. I look forward to traveling by car. It will give me an opportunity to take in many geographical sights. I hope to see the South Carolina beaches, the Georgia islands, and the Florida Keys.

Before I leave, I plan to visit several people whom I will not see for a while. I will visit my grandmother, my friend Gary, and my cousin April. Of course, I will remain in contact with everyone while I am away. I will get in touch with my family and friends in a variety of ways. I will write letters, make phone calls, and e-mail those who have computers.

6. _____

7. _____

8. _____

9. _____

10. _____

Grade 7: Unit 5 Capitalization and Punctuation (Use with pupil book pages 250–251.)
Skill: Students will use colons to combine sentences.

Mechanics

10 Abbreviations

Tuesday	Tues.	February	Feb.
Junior	Jr.	Admiral	Adm.
Post Office	P.O.	Street	St.
Company	Co.	National League	NL
Indiana	IN	Missouri	MO
gallon	gal.	hour	hr

Underline the words that can be abbreviated. Then write their abbreviations. Use your dictionary to help you.

1. The play will be performed in August. _____
2. The shopping center is located on Route 27 near Woodbridge. _____
3. Bob Blake, Registered Nurse, will help you. _____
4. Kenisha watches *Nova* on the Public Broadcasting Service. _____
5. Dexter lives in Galveston, Texas. _____
6. Boil the egg for exactly one minute. _____
7. The highest point in that state is fourteen thousand feet. _____
8. Dora works for Morris and Chadwick, Incorporated. _____
9. Doctor Elsa Gonzales earned her medical degree in 1957. _____
10. In case of rain, the picnic on Sunday will be postponed. _____
11. Please turn to page 105. _____
12. The car was moving 40 miles per hour. _____
13. Will you buy a gallon of milk, please? _____
14. You must turn left at Royal Boulevard. _____
15. General Tool Corporation has opportunities for employment. _____
16. Shall we call the Internal Revenue Service? _____
17. Juliet addressed the card to Baton Rouge, Louisiana. _____
18. We invited Jake Germain Senior to dinner. _____

(continued)

Mechanics

Name _____

10 Abbreviations *(continued from page 108)*

Challenge

Dr. Foy wrote the classified ad below. The local newspaper, however, will not accept ads that are more than 112 letters. Help Dr. Foy rewrite his ad, using abbreviations. Count each punctuation mark as a letter. Use your dictionary to help you.

Motorbike for sale. 25 miles per hour top speed. Write Doctor Jerry Foy, Junior, Post Office Box 42, Coos Bay, Oregon 97420, or come to 15 Mount Adams Boulevard on Wednesday, October 5.

_____

_____

_____

Now write your own ad for something you would like to sell. Use 112 letters or fewer. Include abbreviations wherever possible.

_____

_____

_____

_____

Writing Application: A List ———————————————— DESCRIBING

Suppose that your principal has asked you to make a list of ten places, events, and people in your town or city that would interest visiting foreign students. Use at least one word that can be abbreviated in each item of your list. Underline the word and write its abbreviation.

Grade 7: Unit 5 Capitalization and Punctuation   *(Use with pupil book pages 252–254.)*
Skill: Students will write abbreviations correctly.

WORKBOOK PLUS

Mechanics

Name _____

11 Apostrophes

Possessive Nouns	Contractions
John Roebling's ideas were different.	He didn't use chain cables.
The Roeblings' devotion was remarkable.	They'd finally finish the bridge.
The people's admiration pleased them.	They'll be remembered forever.

A Rewrite each sentence, adding an apostrophe where it is needed.

1. The Brooklyn Bridge is one of John Roeblings masterpieces.
   _____

2. Engineers didnt use wire ropes for bridges until Roebling tried it.
   _____

3. After this designers death, his son Washington took over.
   _____

4. Even then, the bridge almost wasnt finished.
   _____

5. Washington Roebling became ill and couldnt work at the bridge site.
   _____

6. Washingtons wife, Emily, became his spokesperson.
   _____

B 7–12. These headlines have six incorrect or missing apostrophes. Use proofreading marks to correct them.

Example:  Roebling's Death Puts Bridge Project in Peril

Proofreading Marks
- ¶ Indent
- ∧ Add
- ⌐ Delete
- ≡ Capital letter
- / Small letter
- ⌵⌵ Add quotes
- ∧ Add comma
- ⊙ Add period
- ∽ Transpose

Proofreading

Many Designers Plan's Are Rejected for Brooklyn Bridge

Bridge's Cables Wont Break, Claim's Roebling

Emily Roebling Says' Shell Help Finish the Job

(continued)

Mechanics Name _____

11 Apostrophes *(continued from page 110)*

Challenge

A builder remodels a house by adding rooms or by changing the original structure. Remodel each sentence below. Begin by underlining the two nouns in each sentence. Then write a contraction for two other words in the sentence. Be sure to use apostrophes correctly.

Example: She is fixing the <u>furnaces</u> of the <u>welcomers</u>.   _____She's_____

1. The suppers of the victors were not hot.   _____
2. He is wearing the spectacles of the girl.   _____
3. He will auction the jewelry of the monarch.   _____
4. The seats of the animals should not be broken.   _____
5. They did not hear the noises of those dogs.   _____
6. I will buy a volume from my chef.   _____

Now finish remodeling the sentences above. Substitute two nouns that rhyme for each pair of underlined nouns. One of the new nouns must be possessive. Rewrite each sentence using these rhyming nouns and the contraction.

Example: She's fixing the **greeters' heaters**.

1. _____
2. _____
3. _____
4. _____
5. _____
6. _____

Writing Application: A Paragraph

Suppose that you are a bridge designer. Write a paragraph, describing a design for a new type of bridge. Also tell how it will be built. Use a possessive noun or a contraction in each sentence.

Grade 7: Unit 5   Capitalization and Punctuation   *(Use with pupil book pages 255–257.)*
Skill: Students will use apostrophes in possessive nouns and contractions.

Mechanics

Name _____

12 Hyphens, Dashes, and Parentheses

Hyphens	Ben's great-uncle counted forty-seven frogs in the pond.
Dashes	Those frogs—I don't believe it—were all croaking.
Parentheses	The frogs (amphibians) kept us awake.

A Rewrite the sentences, adding hyphens, dashes, and parentheses where they are needed.

1. Ben photographed close ups of frogs and wrote a report about them.

2. When the air reaches sixty five degrees, frogs become active.

3. Frogs almost all of them begin their lives in the water.

4. They change from tadpole to frog in a short time a few weeks.

B 5–8. This part of a student's science report has four problems with hyphens, dashes, and parentheses. Use proofreading marks to correct the report.

Example Amphibians_a class of animals that includes frogs, toads, and salamanders_usually begin life in water.

Proofreading Marks
- ¶ Indent
- ∧ Add
- ℘ Delete
- ≡ Capital letter
- / Small letter
- ⌄⌄ Add quotes
- ∧ Add comma
- ⊙ Add period
- ∽ Transpose

Proofreading

I have twenty two salamanders living in two terrariums fish tanks with soil inside. My salamanders which all have names—beginning with *W*—eat grubs and worms. Last week they ate thirty five grubs and fourteen worms. A salamander that loses a limb (a leg or tail) can regrow it.

(continued)

112 **WORKBOOK PLUS**

Grade 7: Unit 5   Capitalization and Punctuation   (*Use with pupil book pages 258–260.*)
Skill: Students will use hyphens, dashes, and parentheses correctly.

Mechanics

12 Hyphens, Dashes, and Parentheses (continued from page 112)

Challenge

One of Ben's relatives has a fascinating friend. Find out more about his friend. On a separate piece of paper, list all the words in the boxes numbered 1. Then do the same for the words in the boxes numbered 2, 3, 4, and 5.

2 green	1 pets	3 in	2 Croak	4 story	5 insects	2 Her
3 Croak	4 one	5 ants	1 has	2 is	4 years	3 terrarium
2 named	5 and	4 a	3 a	2 pet	3 a	1 interesting
1 aunt	2 it	3 lives	2 is	5 eats	4 old	3 what
4 This	3 name	1 My	5 flies	4 twenty	5 Croak	2 dark
2 favorite	4 likely	2 bullfrog	4 friend	1 great	2 a	4 is

Now write each list of words as a sentence. Add hyphens, dashes, and parentheses where they are needed.

1. _____
2. _____
3. _____
4. _____
5. _____

Writing Application: A Post Card

DESCRIBING

Suppose that you have been observing frogs and snakes at camp. Write a post card to a friend, describing one of your observations. Include hyphens, dashes, and parentheses in your message.

Grammar/Usage

Name _____

1 Pronouns and Antecedents

Minnesota is well known for **its** bitter winters.
Some Minnesotans say **they** wouldn't live **their** lives anywhere else.

A Write each underlined pronoun and its antecedent or antecedents. The antecedent may be in a different sentence.

1. His first winter in St. Paul thrilled Ted. _____

2. Joy and Ann visited him there. _____

3. They wanted to see the St. Paul Winter Carnival. _____

4. Many cities and towns have their biggest festivals in winter. _____

5. The friends went to the St. Paul Winter Carnival. They were excited about the festival. _____

6. Ann said that she would enter the ice-sculpting contest. _____

B 7–12. This newspaper article has six incorrect or missing pronouns. Use proofreading marks to correct the article.

Example: The man living across the street couldn't find ~~their~~ ^his car in the deep snowdrifts.

Proofreading Marks
- ¶ Indent
- ∧ Add
- ⌐ Delete
- ≡ Capital letter
- / Small letter
- ˇˇ Add quotes
- ∧ Add comma
- ⊙ Add period
- ∼ Transpose

Proofreading

Mayor Declares Storm Emergency As It Leaves for Florida

Yesterday a fierce storm blew into New York and New Jersey, leaving a blanket of snow in their path. Thousands of residents lost our power and had to battle huge snowdrifts to get to jobs.

The subways and airport suffered delays on most of them schedules. But Mayor Fred Kay and his family caught an early flight to Miami. "Good luck," they said, "I'll monitor the situation closely."

(continued)

WORKBOOK PLUS

Grade 7: Unit 6 Pronouns *(Use with pupil book pages 280–282.)*
Skill: Students will identify the antecedents of pronouns.

Grammar/Usage

1 Pronouns and Antecedents (continued from page 114)

Challenge

Ted, Joy, and Ann searched the pages of their school newspaper, the *St. Paul Gazette*. They were looking for information about next month's Winter Carnival. The paragraphs below were taken from this newspaper. One pronoun in each paragraph does not have a clear antecedent. Write that pronoun and its antecedent. Use the clues in the paragraph to help you.

  Heavy snowstorms were reported in Minnesota and Wisconsin. Because it was declared a disaster area, the Vikings were unable to play their scheduled football game.

1. _____

  Will the Senators and the House members finish work today? The hundred members hope for an early adjournment because they would like to begin their holiday soon.

2. _____

  The Winter Carnival is only a month away. Auditions for Vulcanus, a fire king, and King Borealis will be held on Friday. He melts the beautiful ice palace at the end of the Carnival. Wouldn't you love to play either role?

3. _____

  Voyager 2 sent back photographs of Saturn and Venus. Scientists were amazed by the thickness of its bands.

4. _____

  Plans for another bridge or tunnel across the St. Croix River were revealed. If built, it would improve the flow of traffic, but the expense of digging the river bottom would be tremendous.

5. _____

  Jane Pauley and Barbara Bush have been invited to the St. Paul Winter Carnival. Unfortunately she hasn't responded yet. The committee hopes to hear from this television anchorwoman soon.

6. _____

Now choose one of the paragraphs above. On a separate piece of paper, rewrite the paragraph so that the antecedent of the pronoun is clear.

Writing Application: A Paragraph

  Write a paragraph titled "Why I Like Winter" or "Why I Dislike Winter." Include at least five pronouns in your paragraph. Draw an arrow from each pronoun to its antecedent.

Grade 7: Unit 6 Pronouns (Use with pupil book pages 280–282.)
Skill: Students will use pronouns and their antecedents correctly.

Revising Strategies: Sentence Fluency

Name _____

Writing Clearly with Pronouns

Unclear sentence	When Tani's dog ran into the lumber pile, it fell over.
Clear sentences	When Tani's dog ran into the lumber pile, **the wood** fell over.
	Tani's dog ran into the lumber pile **and knocked** it over.

Using Pronouns Well 1–5. Revise the description. Replace the unclear pronoun in each underlined sentence, or rearrange the sentence to make the antecedent clear.

Revising

   Armond stepped into the batter's box and squared up to the pitcher. He was concerned, not because the team depended on him for a hit, but because his dad was calling balls and strikes at the plate. <u>He judged the first pitch to be a ball, high and outside the plate.</u> Armond stepped back. <u>He heard him yell, "Stee-rike one."</u> Again he took his stance and swung and missed at a fastball right down the middle. <u>"Stee-rike two," he could hear him roar once more.</u> The next three pitches were balls and Armond now faced a full count.
   Armond settled in against the pitcher. <u>He threw a curve ball that he thought was dropping low and outside.</u> He held his swing. "Stee-rike three," announced the umpire. <u>On the drive home from the game, he told him that he must learn to judge the strike zone better.</u> He showed him two tickets to the World Series and said, "I thought we'd go and pick up some pointers from the pros."

1. _____
   _____

2. _____
   _____

3. _____
   _____

4. _____
   _____

5. _____
   _____

(continued)

Writing Clearly with Pronouns (continued from page 116)

Unclear description	The track shook as the roller coaster began its ascent. Then it started to jerk, and it almost seemed to be moving backward.
Clear description	The track shook as the roller coaster began its ascent. Then **the ride** started to jerk, and **the entire line of cars** seemed to be moving backward.

Avoiding Pronoun Overload 6–10. Revise the underlined sentences. Replace each unclear pronoun either with its antecedent or with a noun or noun phrase.

Revising

Leroy and his Uncle Raul were going to the amusement park on Thursday. <u>He was more than a little concerned about it.</u> He was worried about going on the rides with Uncle Raul. People in the family talked about how bad luck always seemed to follow his uncle. They spoke of that automatic garage door. <u>They described how it came crashing down with Raul's brand new car under it.</u> Then there was last spring. <u>That was the time Raul slipped off his lawn tractor into a ditch and chased after it as it roared through the neighbor's garden.</u>

On another occasion Uncle Raul was on the roof and the ladder fell away from the house, leaving him stranded on the rooftop for hours. As the time grew near, Leroy became more and more nervous. <u>He thought about making up some excuse but he knew he would be disappointed.</u> So, when Thursday came they climbed into the car and started off to the park. Uncle Raul's luck held out. <u>Twenty miles into the trip the car broke down and he gave a sigh of relief.</u>

6. _____
7. _____
_____
8. _____
_____
9. _____
_____
10. _____

2 Personal Pronouns

Person	First　　　　　　　　　second　　　third
	I bought a new computer. Would you like to use it?
Singular	My computer is inexpensive; however, it is a good one.
Plural	Computers save time. They can make a person's job easy.

Underline each pronoun and label it *first*, *second*, or *third* person. Then label it *singular* or *plural*. If it is third person singular, write *masculine*, *feminine*, or *neuter*.

1. A computer can help us in countless ways. _____
2. You should all know about this tool. _____
3. Meg, can you operate a computer? _____
4. Some people consider me an expert. _____
5. I know a lot about computers, but many people don't. _____
6. Meg and Jim wanted to learn word processing, so they took a course. _____
7. The teacher showed them hardware and software. _____
8. Jim asked her the names of some programs. _____
9. Ms. Iba listed them on the board. _____
10. Then she assigned each student a computer. _____
11. Jim took a disk and put it into the disk drive. _____
12. He switched on the monitor. _____
13. Ms. Iba gave him more help. _____
14. Will he be an expert soon? _____
15. All of us will be experts. _____

(continued)

WORKBOOK PLUS

Grade 7: Unit 6 Pronouns *(Use with pupil book pages 285–287.)*
Skill: Students will identify personal pronouns and their person, number, and gender.

Grammar

2 Personal Pronouns (continued from page 118)

Challenge

In the column on the left are the definitions of twelve words. Read each definition and write the word. Then write the personal pronoun that is contained in the word. The personal pronoun that you write must agree with the information given in the computer punch code next to it. Use the key below to help you understand the information given in the punch code.

FIRST PERSON	SECOND PERSON	THIRD PERSON	SINGULAR	PLURAL	MASCULINE	FEMININE	NEUTER
■	■	■	■	■	■	■	■

DEFINITION	WORD	PRONOUN	PUNCH CODE
1. not old	_____	_____	□■□□■□□□
2. climate	_____	_____	□□■□■□□□
3. national song	_____	_____	□□■■□■□□
4. nut's covering	_____	_____	□□■■□□□□
5. robber	_____	_____	□□■□■□□■
6. knitted garment	_____	_____	■□□□□□□□
7. end	_____	_____	■□□□□□□□
8. buyer	_____	_____	■□□□□□□□
9. periodical	_____	_____	■□□□□□□□
10. punctuation mark	_____	_____	□□■■□□□□
11. scissors	_____	_____	□□■■□□□□
12. sewer's finger protection	_____	_____	□□■■□□□□

Writing Application: An Advertisement — PERSUADING

Suppose that you work for an advertising agency. Write an advertisement, promoting a new line of personal computers. Include at least five personal pronouns. Make sure that each pronoun agrees with its antecedent.

Grade 7: Unit 6   Pronouns   (Use with pupil book pages 285–287.)
Skill: Students will use personal pronouns correctly.

3 Subject and Object Pronouns

Subject pronouns	**We** called a travel agent. *(subject)*
	The organizer of the trip was **she**. *(predicate pronoun)*
Object pronouns	Her plans thrilled **them**. *(direct object)*
	She gave **us** excellent information. *(indirect object)*

A Underline the correct pronouns in parentheses to complete the sentences. Then label the underlined pronouns *subject, predicate pronoun, direct object,* or *indirect object.*

1. (I, Me) went to Puerto Rico with my brother. _____
2. (He, Him) didn't have enough money, however. _____
3. Our mother gave (he, him) the necessary money. _____
4. Friends gave (we, us) good advice. _____
5. (They, Them) recommended a visit to Luquillo. _____
6. The people who give the best advice are (they, them)! _____
7. We sent (they, them) post cards. _____
8. Its curving, palm-lined beach amazed (me, I). _____

B 9–14. This thank-you note has six incorrect pronouns. Use proofreading marks to correct the note.

Example: The taxi driver helped we find a nice restaurant. *(us)*

Proofreading Marks
- ¶ Indent
- ∧ Add
- ⌿ Delete
- ≡ Capital letter
- / Small letter
- ⌄⌄ Add quotes
- ⌃ Add comma
- ⊙ Add period
- ∪ Transpose

Proofreading

Dear Diane,

Thanks for introducing I to Martina. Tom was also glad to meet she. Her made us feel at home. Her English and Spanish are very good. Wherever us went, her knew the way. Her knows all the great spots in Madrid!

Sincerely, Caroline

(continued)

Grammar/Usage

Name _____

3 Subject and Object Pronouns (continued from page 120)

Challenge

Figure out the identity of these famous travelers. Fill in the first four blanks with subject or object pronouns. Then write the names of the people. The initials are given to help you.

1. An astronaut am _____. _____ landed on the moon. TV viewers saw _____ plant a flag on its surface. _____ am N_____ A_____.

2. A captain was _____. _____ tried to be the first to sail around the world. Historians give _____ credit for making the voyage. _____ was F_____ M_____.

3. The owner of a silver mine was _____. _____ sailed on the Titanic. _____ survival earned _____ the nickname "Unsinkable." _____ was M_____ B_____.

4. A pilot was _____. _____ was the first woman to fly across the Atlantic. Everyone admired _____. _____ was A_____ E_____.

5. A diplomat, writer, and lecturer was _____. _____ was the wife of a three-term President. World leaders consulted _____. _____ was E_____ R_____.

6. Explorers were _____. Jefferson gave _____ instructions. _____ journeyed through new territories. _____ were M_____ L_____ and W_____ C_____.

Writing Application: A Post Card

Write a post card to a friend, describing a trip that you've taken or hope to take. Describe the people and the things that you saw. Include subject and object pronouns in your message.

Grade 7: Unit 6   Pronouns   (Use with pupil book pages 288–290.)
Skill: Students will use subject and object pronouns correctly.

4 Pronouns in Compound Subjects and Objects

| Compound subject | Gina and **I** are best friends. |
| Compound object | Adam took **her** and **me** to a concert. |

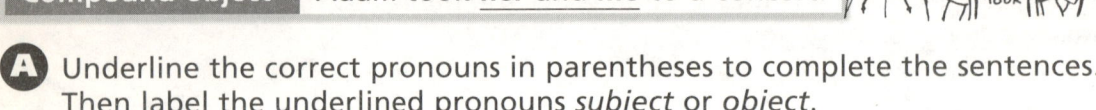

A Underline the correct pronouns in parentheses to complete the sentences. Then label the underlined pronouns *subject* or *object*.

1. My brother Adam and (I, me) have the same birthday. _____

2. (He, Him) and (I, me) are exactly two years apart in age. _____

3. Tina always gives (he, him) and (I, me) a balloon bouquet. _____

4. Our neighbors are Gina and (she, her). _____

5. Gina and (she, her) are identical twins. _____

6. (They, Them) and (we, us) were born on the same day. _____

7. Last year our parents gave (they, them) and (we, us) a party. _____

B 8–14. This e-mail message has seven incorrect pronouns. Use proofreading marks to correct the message.

Example: Eric and ~~her~~ *she* will be showing them how to skate.

Proofreading Marks
- ¶ Indent
- ∧ Add
- ˞ Delete
- ≡ Capital letter
- / Small letter
- ⌄⌄ Add quotes
- ∧ Add comma
- ⊙ Add period
- ∪ Transpose

Proofreading — e-mail

Michael,

My friend Marcus and me are throwing a skating party Friday night at Roll-A-Rink. (Our birthdays are coming and between you and I, he turns 18.) Please call he or I tonight. I want you, your sisters and brothers to Come to Skate and Don't be Late! Don't forget to tell each one to come early and ask them to bring a CD. Say hi to your cousin and her boyfriend. Him and her can really skate.

Keyshawn

(continued)

Grade 7: Unit 6 Pronouns (Use with pupil book pages 291–292.)
Skill: Students will use pronouns in compound subjects and compound objects.

Usage   Name _____

4 Pronouns in Compound Subjects and Objects

(continued from page 122)

Challenge

Gina noted the birthdays of some of her classmates on the calendar pages below. She also listed a possible present for each person.

Write four sentences telling about Gina's friends' birthdays and the gifts that Gina plans to give. In each sentence use one or more pronouns in a compound subject or a compound object. Circle your compound pronoun. Above the pronoun, write *subject* or *object*.

_____
_____
_____
_____
_____
_____
_____
_____

Writing Application: Paragraph

Think about a memorable birthday. It could be yours, or someone else's. What made that birthday special? Write a paragraph about the birthday. Remember to use vivid visual details and to include emotional language so that the reader can really understand what happened. Include sentences containing pronouns in a compound subject or compound object.

Grade 7: Unit 6 Pronouns *(Use with pupil book pages 291–292.)*
Skill: Students will use pronouns in compound subjects and compound objects.

Grammar/Usage

5 Possessive Pronouns

Before Nouns	Stand Alone
Our trees are beautiful.	Those trees are **ours**.
Your fence divides the yard.	The fence is **yours**.

A Write the correct words in parentheses to complete the sentences.

1. What things are (your, yours) and what things are (my, mine)? _____

2. (Its, It's) not always an easy question. _____

3. Suppose I have an apple tree in (my, mine) back yard. _____

4. (Its, It's) branches shade my neighbor's garden. _____

5. Are the branches that are over (her, hers) yard (her, hers) to trim? _____

6. Suppose an apple tree stands in (your, yours) yard. _____

7. (Your, Yours) neighbors pick apples from the limbs over (they're, their) land. _____

8. (Their, They're) not questions with clear answers! _____

B 9–12. There are four errors with pronouns in this paragraph. Use proofreading marks to correct the errors in the paragraph.

Example: Lawyers have debated issues of fairness throughout ours̸ history.

Proofreading Marks
- ¶ Indent
- ∧ Add
- ⌒ Delete
- ≡ Capital letter
- / Small letter
- ⌃⌄ Add quotes
- ⌃ Add comma
- ⊙ Add period
- ∽ Transpose

Proofreading

Suppose your the owner of an apple tree with branches in you're neighbors' yard. What if the apples drop in they're yard? Are the apples yours? Or are the apples there's? If you were the lawyer, what would you do?

(continued)

Grammar/Usage

Name _____

5 Possessive Pronouns (continued from page 124)

Challenge

Marcy, Nanette, Olaf, and Paolo own different colored cars. Figure out the color of each owner's car. Use the chart and the clues to help you. Place an X under each category that you eliminate. Then draw a star in the box that shows the color of each person's car.

	White	Red	Gray	Yellow
Marcy				
Nanette				
Olaf				
Paolo				

CLUES
- On Monday Nanette and Olaf went to a concert with the owner of the white car.
- Paolo saw the owners of the red car and the gray car at the supermarket yesterday.
- The owner of the yellow car thinks that his car is more luxurious than Marcy's or Paolo's car.
- Nanette's car is not a bright color.

Now write four sentences about the car owners and their cars. In each sentence include the name of each car owner and the color of his or her car. Try to use a different possessive pronoun in each sentence.

1. _____
2. _____
3. _____
4. _____

Writing Application: A Paragraph

Have you ever been in an argument about who owned something or who had a right to use it? Write a paragraph, describing the argument. Who were the people involved, and how was the argument resolved? Use at least five different possessive pronouns in your paragraph.

Grade 7: Unit 6 Pronouns (Use with pupil book pages 293–295.)
Skill: Students will use possessive pronouns correctly.

Grammar/Usage

Name _____

6 Interrogative Pronouns

What was the detective's first clue?
Which of the clues can be discarded?
Who handles this kind of case?
Whom should we hire to investigate?
Whose is this address book?

A Write the interrogative pronoun in each sentence.

1. Whom should we call first? _____
2. Who located the owner of the mansion? _____
3. Which of the alarms were disconnected? _____
4. Whose was the helicopter on the roof? _____
5. What is the official explanation? _____

B Write *who, whom, whose,* or *who's* to complete each sentence.

6. _____ investigating this mystery?
7. _____ will the detective ask for help?
8. _____ did the detective question?
9. _____ has an alibi?
10. _____ found this evidence?
11. _____ are the tools in the living room?
12. _____ were the fingerprints on the window?
13. _____ are the footprints in the back yard?
14. _____ noticed the empty cabinet?
15. _____ did the cook see in the courtyard?
16. _____ witnessed the argument in the library?
17. _____ telling the best story?
18. _____ the chief suspect?

(continued)

126 **WORKBOOK PLUS**
▲■

Grade 7: Unit 6 Pronouns (Use with pupil book pages 296–298.)
Skill: Students will identify interrogative pronouns and will use *who, whom, whose,* and *who's* correctly.

Grammar/Usage   Name _____

6 Interrogative Pronouns (continued from page 126)

Challenge

Read the sentences in the boxes below. Then number them to show the proper time sequence.

| _____ He told the worried farmers what they should do. | | _____ The farms belonging to Sy Lowe, Al Falfa, and Otis Fields were hardest hit. Al Falfa knew what to do. |

| _____ It was Gomer's idea to spread eighty tons of aspirin over the sickly hay fields. | _____ Hay fever struck Mudd County yesterday. | _____ Al called hay expert Diz Gomer. Diz took the temperature of the stricken hay. |

Now write five questions that can be answered by the sentences in the numbered boxes. Use a different interrogative pronoun in each question.

1. _____
2. _____
3. _____
4. _____
5. _____

Writing Application: A List

Kitty Benson has lost Katrina, her prized feline. Was it catnapped? Suppose that you are a private detective hired to handle this catastrophe. List nine questions that you might ask a suspect. Use each interrogative pronoun at least once.

Grade 7: Unit 6 Pronouns (Use with pupil book pages 296–298.)
Skill: Students will use interrogative pronouns correctly.

Grammar/Usage

7 Demonstrative Pronouns

This is the gangplank.
These are the tickets for the boat ride.
That is our tour boat at the pier.
Those are the crew members over there.

Write the correct demonstrative pronoun in parentheses to complete each sentence. Then underline the noun pointed out by the demonstrative pronoun.

1. (This, These) is a spectacular event. _____
2. Are (these, those) the sailboats on the horizon? _____
3. (These, Those) are tugboats there at the head of the parade. _____
4. (This, That) is the skyline of Boston in the distance. _____
5. (These, Those) are buoys on the other side of the channel. _____
6. (This, These) is a hundred-year-old vessel. _____
7. (These, Those) are the officials on the farthest pier. _____
8. (This, That) is a schooner we have rented. _____
9. (This, That) is the captain over there. _____
10. (This, These) are the quarters for the crew. _____
11. Is (this, these) the galley? _____
12. (This, That) is a lighthouse beyond the buoy. _____
13. (That, Those) are obviously new sails. _____
14. (This, These) are the wooden masts. _____
15. (This, That) is a sailor at the top of the mast. _____
16. (This, These) are the flags of several nations. _____
17. Is (this, these) the largest ship in the parade? _____
18. (This, These) is the *U.S.S. Constitution*. _____

(continued)

Grammar/Usage   Name _____

7 Demonstrative Pronouns (continued from page 128)

Challenge

Write sentences that tell what the characters in each cartoon are saying. Use a different demonstrative pronoun in each sentence.

Writing Application: Sentences — INFORMING

Suppose that you are a newscaster at a parade or a sports event. Write six sentences, introducing the participants. Begin each sentence with a demonstrative pronoun. Use each of the four demonstrative pronouns.

Grade 7: Unit 6   Pronouns   (Use with pupil book pages 299–301.)
Skill: Students will use demonstrative pronouns in sentences.

Usage

Name _____

8 Indefinite Pronouns

Singular	**Everybody** in school <u>watches</u> the show. **All** of the action <u>takes</u> place in a boarding school.
Plural	**Few** of us ever <u>see</u> live productions. **All** of the actors <u>gather</u> their materials.

A Underline each indefinite pronoun. Then label the pronoun *singular* or *plural*.

1. All of us are enjoying our visit to the station. _____

2. Few have ever been inside a studio. _____

3. Someone explains the job to each worker. _____

4. Many have experience in television. _____

5. Everybody in the TV studio is quiet. _____

6. One of the boom operators moves a microphone. _____

7. Some of the monitors have been turned on. _____

8. Each of the production assistants signals the director. _____

B 9–14. There are six errors with verbs that agree with indefinite pronouns in this student's notes. Use proofreading marks to correct the errors in the notes.

Proofreading Marks
- ¶ Indent
- ∧ Add
- ꝏ Delete
- ≡ Capital letter
- / Small letter
- ⌄⌄ Add quotes
- ⌃ Add comma
- ⊙ Add period
- ∽ Transpose

Example: One of the students take^s notes for the school newspaper.

Proofreading

At first, everything proceed on schedule.

Most of the scenes has already been taped.

Then several of the actors forgets their lines. Somebody prompt

the performers. The director says that some needs another

rehearsal. Everyone takes a break, but no one leave the station.

(continued)

130 WORKBOOK PLUS Grade 7: Unit 6 Pronouns *(Use with pupil book pages 302–305.)*
Skill: Students will identify singular and plural indefinite pronouns and will choose verbs and pronouns to agree with them.

Usage

8 Indefinite Pronouns (continued from page 130)

Challenge

William Archibald Spooner had a habit of switching sounds at the beginnings of words. These slips of the tongue became known as "spoonerisms." Look at the example.

Example: Everybody competes in **r**oday's **t**ace.
(Everybody competes in today's race.)

Below are some spoonerisms by a local television announcer. Write what you think the announcer really meant to say. Be sure to correct all mistakes in agreement.

1. Something were filmed in whack and blite.

2. Most of the demonstrators left with its ligns sowered.

3. Several of the wen and mimmen performs without her cue cards.

4. Everyone in these towns look forward to the sourist teason.

5. One seldom make a half-warmed fish.

6. All of the spectators was forced into the roaring pain.

7. Neither of the contestants know Hoobert Heever.

Writing Application: A Review — INFORMING

Suppose that you are a television critic for a local newspaper. Write a review of a new situation comedy, a documentary, or a drama. Use at least six indefinite pronouns in your review. Be sure that the verbs and the personal pronouns agree with the indefinite pronouns.

Grade 7: Unit 6   Pronouns   *(Use with pupil book pages 302–305.)*
  Skill: Students will write verbs and pronouns to agree with indefinite pronouns.

Grammar/Usage   Name _____

9 Reflexive and Intensive Pronouns

| Reflexive | The students considered **themselves** lucky. |
| Intensive | Mr. Barron **himself** conducted the class. |

A Underline the correct pronoun in parentheses to complete each sentence. Then label it *intensive* or *reflexive*.

1. My classmates recorded (themselves, theirselves) on videotape. _____

2. The equipment (itself, it) was fascinating. _____

3. The instructor, Mr. Barron, supplied most of it (hisself, himself). _____

4. The camera (it, itself) belonged to the school. _____

5. Have you ever seen (you, yourself) on TV? _____

6. Sharon had never even heard (she, herself) on a tape recorder. _____

7. I prepared (me, myself) for a shock! _____

B Underline the correct pronoun in parentheses to complete each sentence. Then write its antecedent.

8. A few students settled (theirselves, themselves) in front of the TV screen. _____

9. The tape (itself, it) lasted an hour. _____

10. We all studied (us, ourselves) intently. _____

11. Anita considered (she, herself) too thin. _____

12. Rick watched (hisself, himself) intently and made no comment. _____

13. Some people were uncomfortable watching (theirselves, themselves) on TV. _____

14. Sharon (she, herself) couldn't look! _____

15. It occurred to Ron that (he, himself) might enjoy a career in television. _____

16. I (myself, me) was pleased with my TV image. _____

(continued)

132 WORKBOOK PLUS   Grade 7: Unit 6   Pronouns (Use with pupil book pages 306–308.)
Skill: Students will identify and will use reflexive and intensive pronouns.

Grammar/Usage

Name _____

9 Reflexive and Intensive Pronouns (continued from page 132)

Challenge

An idiom is an expression that has a meaning different from the meaning of the individual words. The cartoons below illustrate some common idioms. Each idiom contains a reflexive pronoun.

Now read these comments made by students after a classroom videotaping. Complete each comment by writing an idiom shown in one of the cartoons above. Remember that each idiom you write must include a reflexive pronoun.

1. I did such a terrible job that I _____ .

2. Don't be so nervous. You must _____ .

3. They _____ trying to perfect their act.

4. She _____ because she wasn't paying attention.

5. Bert is so vain. He's always _____ .

6. She worked so hard that she _____ .

Now choose four of the reflexive pronouns that you used above. On a separate piece of paper, write four sentences, using each of these pronouns as an intensive pronoun.

Writing Application: A Paragraph

The poet Robert Burns wished for the gift "to see ourselves as others see us." Do you think that this would be a good idea? Write a paragraph, telling why or why not. Use at least three reflexive or intensive pronouns in your paragraph.

Grade 7: Unit 6 Pronouns (Use with pupil book pages 306–308.)
Skill: Students will use reflexive and intensive pronouns in sentences.

Homophones

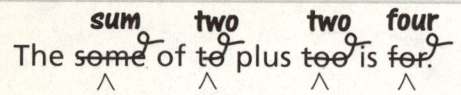

1–10. Replace each incorrect homophone with the correct word. Use the list of homophones and their definitions in the box for help.

more increased amount	**sea** body of water
moor wasteland	**see** observe, view
to until, as far as	**wait** pause, hesitate
too also	**weight** heaviness, density
made created, formed, built	**for** in favor of, in order to
maid household worker	**four** whole number between 3 and 5
night evening, dusk to dawn	**I** reference to oneself
knight horseman, gentleman	**eye** organ of sight
week seven days	**by** through, near, close to
weak having no strength	**buy** purchase

Revising

After Jason saw a TV show on self-motivation, he wanted to learn moor about it. So he went too the library and took out several books on the subject.

He spent the next weak practicing the techniques. Buy concentrating on his breathing, Jason discovered he could enter a state that maid him feel relaxed. His mom had asked him four many days to clean his room. Perhaps these techniques would help him do it.

That knight Jason concentrated so hard that he fell asleep. Upon waking, he was astonished to sea that his room was spotless. "It worked!" Jason thought. Then his mother came in and announced that he was grounded. "When I gave you one more chance to clean your room last night, you just went to sleep. I couldn't weight any longer, so eye cleaned it myself!"

1 Prepositional Phrases

```
           preposition         object
               |                 |
The group gathered outside the crowded lodge.
                         |
                  prepositional phrase
```

Write each prepositional phrase. Underline the preposition once. Underline the object of the preposition twice.

1. Ms. Engle's class traveled to Colorado on a ski trip.

2. The students learned about ski equipment before the trip.

3. Skis are made from plastics and other materials.

4. Skiers use poles for balance during a ski run.

5. Sandra sat next to Carlos and Mary on the lift.

6. The students went up the lift and down the slopes.

7. On the other side of the mountain were beautiful trails.

8. In front of them were deep woods with many tall pines.

9. The skiers went down the slopes with their instructor.

10. They took lessons from her for two hours.

(continued)

Grade 7: Unit 7 Prepositional Phrases (Use with pupil book pages 326–329.)
Skill: Students will identify prepositional phrases, prepositions, and objects of prepositions.

Grammar

1 Prepositional Phrases (continued from page 135)

Challenge

Sometimes you may want to write rhyming words within a sentence. Study these example sentences that contain prepositional phrases.

Examples: An icy **snowball** flew across the **hall**.
Heather went walking despite the weather.

Write one or more prepositional phrases to complete each sentence below. Make sure at least two words in each sentence rhyme.

1. An early snowstorm delighted Paul _____
2. Icicles on the eaves dripped _____
3. Myra and Jay had fun _____
4. Icy winds blew hard _____
5. Snow clouds gathered high _____
6. The snowplow got stuck _____
7. Snow and sleet fell at my feet _____
8. Cindy rode on a sled _____
9. An anxious Phil raced _____
10. Everyone had a good time _____

Writing Application: A Description

Write five sentences that describe an imaginary ski race or other winter sport that you are watching. Use at least one prepositional phrase in each sentence.

2 Pronouns After Prepositions

Object pronouns Ruben paddled behind **them** and **me**.
I sat between **him** and **her**.

A If the prepositional phrase is incorrect, rewrite the sentence correctly. If the sentence is correct, write *correct*.

1. Mr. and Mrs. Johnson discussed the trip with Ruben and I.

2. The canoe was big enough for me, Ruben, and them.

3. The Johnsons prepared food for we and the others.

4. Canoeing is a lot of fun for I and the Johnsons.

5. I always enjoy trips with the Garcias and they.

B 6–8. There are three errors with object pronouns in this post card. Use proofreading marks to correct the errors.

Example: What is the difference between ~~they~~ ^them and the loons?

Proofreading

Dear Natalie,

Our kayaking trip was terrific! Paddling through the rapids was not difficult for Sam and I. Sue and Ben needed more practice. We traveled along the riverbank. The guide explained the ecology to we and the others. A heron gazed at Sam and I for a very long time.   Love, Charlotte

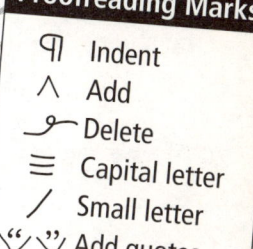

Proofreading Marks
¶ Indent
∧ Add
⤴ Delete
≡ Capital letter
/ Small letter
❞❞ Add quotes
∧ Add comma
⊙ Add period
∽ Transpose

(continued)

Grammar/Usage

2 Pronouns After Prepositions (continued from page 137)

Challenge

Imagine that you write an advice column for the newspaper. You have received the letter shown below. First, cross out each pronoun that is used incorrectly and write the correct pronoun above it. Then, on a separate piece of paper, answer the letter. Use pronouns as objects of prepositions.

Dear Problem Solver,

I hope you can solve a problem for I and my family. Last week my uncle sent a present to we. Two packages arrived with four live lobsters inside of they! What a surprise this was for we and the mail carrier!

Unpacking the lobsters wasn't difficult for my mom and I, but my little sister and brother didn't like looking at they. We had to promise not to let the lobsters near he or she. The lobsters wouldn't fit in the refrigerator. What could we do with they?

Finally, an idea came to my mom and I. We put the lobsters in the bathtub. The problem came later for me and my mom. When we looked for the lobsters at dinner time, we found my sister and brother playing with they. The lobsters had become favorite pets for he and she. We couldn't possibly take the lobsters with we to cook. My sister and brother burst into tears at the suggestion.

Please tell me what to do about he, she, and the lobsters. Also, please hurry with your answer. No one can use the bathtub until you solve this difficult problem for me and my family!

Sincerely,
Cris Tayshun

Writing Application: A Personal Narrative

Write a personal narrative about an activity that you and your friends have participated in outdoors. The activity could be a sport, a community function, or a trip. Include at least four prepositional phrases in which pronouns are the objects of the prepositions.

3 Adjective Phrases

| Adjective phrases | The history **of moving pictures** is interesting.
Creating an illusion **of people in motion** was difficult. |

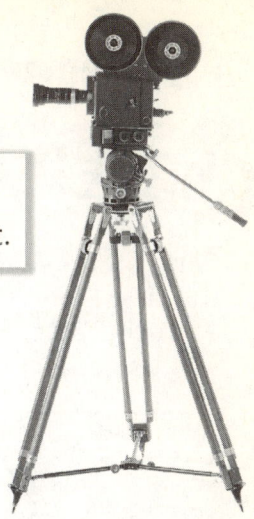

Write each adjective phrase and the word that it modifies.

1. Early photographers could film only posed phases of movement.

2. A number of scientists from France created devices that made pictures move.

3. An inventor photographed a racehorse in action.

4. He used twenty-four different cameras with strings on their shutters.

5. Edison's research on motion pictures is famous.

6. Edison produced a camera with a revolving shutter in front of the film.

7. Edison's kinetoscope contained about fifty feet of film on spools.

8. Edison opened a shop with two rows of coin-operated kinetoscopes.

9. Later, Edison presented the first public exhibit of motion pictures.

10. One of the films showed scenes from a prizefight.

(continued)

Grammar

Name _____

3 Adjective Phrases (continued from page 139)

Challenge

Can you make a still picture come to life? Suppose that the picture below is the first scene in a movie. Write a dialogue for the characters. First, identify each character by using an adjective phrase. Then write what the characters say. Use adjective phrases in your dialogue.

Examples: **Woman near Camel:** Could you give us directions to the nearest oasis?
Man in Turban: Most of the oases in the area have gone dry!

_____
_____
_____
_____
_____
_____
_____

Writing Application: An Application

Most inventors apply for a patent from the government for their new inventions. The patent assures inventors that no one else will be able to use their idea. Suppose that you have just invented a new video camera. Write an application for a patent. Describe the camera and the motion pictures that it can make. Use an adjective phrase in each sentence.

Grade 7: Unit 7 Prepositional Phrases (Use with pupil book pages 333–335.)
Skill: Students will use adjective phrases in sentences.

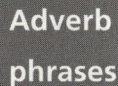

4 Adverb Phrases

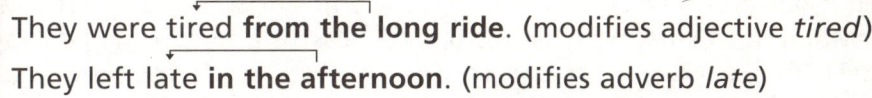

| Adverb phrases | The Gadskis traveled **by car**. (modifies verb *traveled*)
They were tired **from the long ride**. (modifies adjective *tired*)
They left late **in the afternoon**. (modifies adverb *late*) |

Write each adverb phrase and the word or words that it modifies.

1. Last Saturday the Gadskis went on vacation.

2. They traveled across the Green Mountains to Montpelier.

3. Montpelier is located in northern Vermont.

4. The capital is famous for its beautiful location.

5. During one afternoon the Gadskis visited the Shelburne Museum.

6. The Gadskis rode on a ferry across Lake Champlain.

7. Later in the day, they traveled through quaint towns.

8. With enthusiasm and energy, they hiked the Long Trail.

9. They ate a picnic lunch at noon.

10. After a while the Gadskis climbed down the mountain.

(continued)

Grade 7: Unit 7   Prepositional Phrases   *(Use with pupil book pages 336–339.)*
Skill: Students will identify adverb phrases and the words that they modify.

Grammar

4 Adverb Phrases (continued from page 141)

Challenge

Suppose that you are advising friends who are about to go on a cross-country bike tour. Make a list of suggestions for a successful and safe trip. Complete each suggestion below with an adverb phrase. Then write four more suggestions of your own, including an adverb phrase in each one.

1. Carry a water bottle _____
2. Always ride _____
3. Start out early _____
4. Walk your bicycle _____
5. Stop _____
6. Rest frequently _____
7. _____
8. _____
9. _____
10. _____

Writing Application: A Travel Log

Write a brief description of one of the fifty states that you have visited. Describe the things that you saw or the people that you met. Use at least one adverb phrase in each sentence.

Grammar/Usage

Name _____

5 Placing Phrases Correctly

Misplaced	A movie about wildlife is at our local theater **in Africa**.
Correct	A movie about wildlife **in Africa** is at our local theater.

A Rewrite each sentence, changing the position of each misplaced prepositional phrase.

1. The director suggested that we make a movie with a mustache.
   _____

2. The writer with a surprise ending composed a good script.
   _____

3. Students tried out for various roles with acting experience.
   _____

B 4–8. There are five prepositional phrases that are placed incorrectly in this movie review. Use proofreading marks to correct the review.

Example: The filming of the scene attracted a large crowd (in the spacecraft).

Proofreading Marks
- ¶ Indent
- ∧ Add
- ℘ Delete
- ≡ Capital letter
- / Small letter
- ⌄⌄ Add quotes
- ⌃ Add comma
- ⊙ Add period
- ∽ Transpose

Proofreading

Race to Space Race Today

Don't wait another minute with your friends to see *Space Race*! This briskly paced action movie is filled with surprises about falling meteors. The computerized special effects take you in a way you'll never forget through space. And the performances by Ima Starr and Ray Uflight are their best yet! Their final scene is unforgettable on Jupiter. This gifted young director beyond our wildest dreams has created a smash hit!

(continued)

Grade 7: Unit 7 Prepositional Phrases *(Use with pupil book pages 340–342.)*
Skill: Students will revise sentences containing misplaced prepositional phrases.

Grammar/Usage

Name _____

5 Placing Phrases Correctly (continued from page 143)

Challenge

A description of the opening scene of a movie is printed on the filmstrips below. However, the words and phrases are not in the right order. Suppose that you are a film editor. First, color the frames that contain prepositional phrases. Then number the frames to show the order in which they would appear in a sentence.

1.	2.	3.	4.
of brick	approached	the approach	inside the walls
with high towers	on horseback	a man	alerted the people
a wall	the entrance	watched	on the bridge
surrounded	travelers	in ragged clothes	to the danger
a castle	with caution	of the intruders	the sound of horses' hoofs

Now, on a separate piece of paper, write a sentence for each filmstrip, putting the words and phrases in their numbered order. Be sure to place the adjective and adverb phrases correctly.

Writing Application: A Film Review

Suppose that you are a film critic. Write a brief review of a film you have seen recently. Include an adjective phrase or adverb phrase in each sentence. Be sure to place each phrase correctly.

Revising Strategies: Sentence Fluency

Writing with Prepositional Phrases

Choppy sentences	Because of the rain, the players ran off the field. They ran into the dugout.
Combined sentence	Because of the rain, the players ran off the field into the dugout.

Combining Sentences 1–6. Revise the description. Move or create a prepositional phrase to combine each pair of underlined sentences.

Revising

Rugby football is played around the world. More than one hundred countries participate. To many Americans, Rugby appears to have no set rules. The players seem to run, drop kick, and pass the ball at will. This is not the case. Each team consists of fifteen players. No substitutions are allowed. The rules of rugby are very clear. The game is divided into two forty-minute halves. There are no time-outs. A touchdown is worth five points followed by a kick through the opponent's goal worth two points. A three-point goal can be made. It can be scored by a drop kick.

Two major rules control how the ball is moved. The rules relate to the playing field. First, players may not pass the ball forward. Second, a player cannot touch the ball if it was last touched by a teammate. The teammate is running behind him.

1. _____
2. _____
3. _____
4. _____
5. _____
6. _____

(continued)

Grade 7: Unit 7 Prepositional Phrases *(Use with pupil book pages 343–344.)*
Skill: Students will use prepositional phrases to combine sentences.

Revising Strategies: Sentence Fluency

Writing with Prepositional Phrases (continued from page 145)

Without detail	Some music affects our emotions.
With detail	Some music **on the radio** affects our emotions.

Elaborating Sentences 7–14. Revise the paragraph. Elaborate each underlined expression by adding a new prepositional phrase. Use your imagination and your own experience to help.

Revising

Last night we went to a concert. We decided to take public transportation. Our entire family was dressed. At the concert hall we noticed many of the patrons staring. We could not imagine what they were watching. Just then my sister began laughing. She could not stop giggling as she pointed to the huge lollipop. I must have sat on it on the bus. I yanked the lollipop off and took a seat. I am happy to say there were no more embarrassing incidents. We all enjoyed the music.

6 Choosing Correct Prepositions

Tom sat **between** Becky and Huck.
Among Twain's novels, *The Adventures of Huckleberry Finn* is my favorite.
Huck's fishing pole lay on the ground **beside** him.
Besides writing novels, Twain also wrote short stories.

A If the sentence contains an incorrect preposition, rewrite the sentence correctly. If the sentence is correct, write *correct*.

1. I keep this biography of Mark Twain besides my desk.

2. Twain wrote many great works between 1869 and 1910.

3. Between his many characters, Tom Sawyer was one of the most vivid.

4. Besides being an author, Twain was also a riverboat captain.

5. Beside writing and lecturing, Twain also enjoyed traveling.

B 6–8. This paragraph from a book report has three errors with incorrect prepositions. Use proofreading marks to correct the book report.

Example: Put your book report besides the folder.

Proofreading Marks
¶ Indent
∧ Add
⌿ Delete
≡ Capital letter
/ Small letter
⌄⌄ Add quotes
⌃ Add comma
⊙ Add period
∽ Transpose

Proofreading

Among Huck Finn and Tom Sawyer, I like Huck better.

Beside being funny, he gets himself out of many scrapes.

Between all of Twain's characters, I most admire Jim. Besides teaching

Huck many things, he is a true friend.

(continued)

Grade 7: Unit 7 Prepositional Phrases (Use with pupil book pages 345–347.)
Skill: Students will use the prepositions *between, among, beside,* and *besides* correctly.

WORKBOOK PLUS 147

Grammar/Usage

Name _____

6 Choosing Correct Prepositions (continued from page 147)

Challenge

Suppose that you are writing an article for your school newspaper. The article describes a new library that just opened in your school. Study the picture below. Then complete the description of the library. Use the words *between*, *among*, *beside*, and *besides* in your sentences.

1. You can find the nonfiction sections _____
   _____.

2. A large globe is located _____.

3. _____, the library also has a computer.

4. An atlas can be found _____

5. A magazine rack stands _____.

6. _____

7. _____

8. _____

Writing Application: A Letter

Suppose that a friend has asked you to recommend a book. Write a brief letter about a book you have read recently. Use the prepositions *between*, *among*, *beside*, and *besides*.

148 WORKBOOK PLUS

Grade 7: Unit 7 Prepositional Phrases (Use with pupil book pages 345–347.)
Skill: Students will use the prepositions *between*, *among*, *beside*, and *besides* correctly.

Revising Strategies: Vocabulary

Name _____

Idioms

>   angry
> The citizens are still ~~up in arms~~ about the increase in taxes.

1–8. Match each underlined idiom with its meaning in the box. Then rewrite the paragraph so that it expresses the same ideas without using idioms.

| make a strong effort | impossible | upset | all I could take |
| discourage you | take a chance | be quiet | likely to happen |

Revising

    I wasn't sure I could get on the team; however, on the day of tryouts I decided to take the bull by the horns. At first, making the varsity basketball team seemed out of the question. Later, I realized I should throw caution to the wind and try my best.
    At tryouts my stomach was tied in knots. Everyone was screaming as the players took turns shooting baskets from the three-point line. The coach finally said to pipe down and let the players concentrate. As I walked up to the three-point line, a player whispered, "I don't want to rain on your parade, kid, but you don't have a chance." That was the last straw. I was determined to make the team.
    I guess success was in the cards. Today I leave for college on a full basketball scholarship.

Grade 7: Unit 7 Prepositional Phrases   (Use with pupil book page 348.)
     Skill: Students will replace idioms with more precise meanings.

Grammar

1 Clauses

Phrase	**after** the voyage
Clause	subject | predicate **after** Drake saw it
Independent clause	he sighted California
Subordinate clause	**when** he sighted California

Write the underlined group of words. Label it *phrase*, *independent clause*, or *subordinate clause*.

1. <u>After a long sailing voyage</u>, Sir Francis Drake claimed California for England.

2. Spain colonized California <u>after 1600</u>.

3. Spaniards established missions there <u>in the late 1700s</u>.

4. <u>After Mexico won independence</u>, California became part of Mexico.

5. In the 1800s <u>American settlers traveled to California</u>.

6. <u>During the gold rush</u>, thousands of people flocked to California.

7. When they settled in California, <u>some miners became farmers</u>.

8. <u>Because it has an excellent climate</u>, people still move to California.

(continued)

WORKBOOK PLUS Grade 7: Unit 8 Complex Sentences (Use with pupil book pages 362–364.)
Skill: Students will identify phrases, independent clauses, and subordinate clauses.

Grammar

1 Clauses (continued from page 150)

Challenge

How did your town, city, or state get its name? Make up a fictional story or write a factual account, explaining where the name came from. Write one subordinate clause and one independent clause to complete each sentence below. Finish the story with three sentences of your own. Each sentence should contain one subordinate clause and one independent clause.

1. Before the _____,
   _____.

2. Because _____,
   _____.

3. As soon as _____,
   _____.

4. Whenever _____,
   _____.

5. After _____,
   _____.

6. _____
7. _____
8. _____

Writing Application: A Paragraph — INFORMING

Write a paragraph about an important historical or current event that has taken place in your state or province. You might write about the construction of a famous building, an important election, or a special invention. Use at least three subordinate clauses and three phrases.

Grade 7: Unit 8 Complex Sentences (Use with pupil book pages 362–364.)
Skill: Students will use phrases, subordinate clauses, and independent clauses in sentences.

Grammar

2 Compound and Complex Sentences

Simple sentence	independent Admiral Peary discovered the North Pole.
Compound sentence	independent ___ independent It was a difficult trip, but he reached his goal.
Complex sentence	independent ___ subordinate Others may have reached the North Pole before he did.

Copy each sentence. Underline each independent clause. Then label the sentence *simple, compound,* or *complex*.

1. Robert Edwin Peary was an American explorer.

2. While Peary served in the navy, he made geographical surveys.

3. After Peary served as a surveyor, he became an explorer.

4. Although most of his experience had been in warmer climates, in 1886 Peary traveled to Greenland, where it was extremely cold.

5. Peary returned home, and he and others publicized the need for Arctic exploration.

6. The Arctic drew many explorers, and Peary was among them.

7. After several attempts he reached the North Pole.

8. The North Pole remains an important region for exploration.

(continued)

Grammar

2 Compound and Complex Sentences (continued from page 152)

Challenge

Suppose you were with Admiral Peary during his travels to the North Pole. For three days you took the notes below, telling about your daily activities. Use these notes to write a journal entry about the three days. Include three compound sentences and three complex sentences in your journal entry.

Tuesday
checked equipment
met with Peary
discussed strategies
counted supplies
ship harmed by ice

Wednesday
left ship at Ellesmere Island
set up base camp
packed sledges
eager to begin

Thursday
met with native guides
course set over ice fields of Arctic Ocean
will supplies last?

_____
_____
_____
_____
_____
_____
_____
_____
_____

Writing Application: A Report — INFORMING

Suppose that you are a television news reporter. You have learned that an important discovery has just been made. Write a short report about this discovery for the evening news program. Include at least two compound sentences and two complex sentences.

Grade 7: Unit 8 Complex Sentences (Use with pupil book pages 365–367.)
Skill: Students will write simple, compound, and complex sentences.

Revising Strategies: Sentence Fluency

Name _____

Forming Complex and Compound-Complex Sentences

Simple sentences	The lion lives on the plains. It is known as the king of the jungle.
Complex sentence	**Although** the lion lives on the plains, it is known as the king of the jungle.

Combining Sentences: Complex Sentences Combine each pair of underlined sentences into a complex sentence. Use a subordinating conjunction such as *if, although, when, after,* or *because*.

Revising

Lions can roam free in open country. Their coats blend in well with rocks and sand. A lion's life span is considerably less than that of a human. Most lions live about 20 years. Some can live for 30 years. Baby lions are known as cubs. The cubs get older. They follow their mother. As they get older, lions change in physical appearance. A male lion grows a mane. It reaches its third birthday. You may not get the opportunity to see lions in their natural habitat. You visit the zoo. You can observe lions. You probably won't find them in cages. Most zoos today keep animals in natural settings.

1. _____
2. _____
3. _____
4. _____
5. _____
6. _____

(continued)

Grade 7: Unit 8 Complex Sentences (Use with pupil book pages 368–369.)
Skill: Students will combine sentences to form complex sentences using subordinating conjunctions.

Forming Complex and Compound-Complex Sentences

(continued from page 154)

Simple sentences	The roof had caved in. They decided to tear down the old shack. They brought in the bulldozers.
Combined compound-complex sentence	They brought in the bulldozer, and they decided to tear down the old shack because the roof had caved in.

Combining Sentences: Compound-Complex Sentences Revise each set of underlined sentences. Combine simple sentences and use subordinating conjunctions to show relationships between ideas.

Revising

The summer ended. Vicious carpenter ants attacked the old oak tree. Today was the day they would finally take it down. Tara watched as the workers strung cable through the dense branches to hold them in place. That tree had been there as long as Tara could remember. She did not want to see it go. It was in danger of toppling onto the house. Her mind filled with fond memories. Tara and her brother were children. They had built a tree house. They had spent many nights there spinning tales that scared them out of their wits.

Suddenly, the roar of a chain saw and the sound of cracking wood interrupted Tara's thoughts. The branches were swaying. Tara walked into the house. She could not bear to see the tree fall. Within hours it was gone. The next morning Tara noticed how much more sunlight streamed into her room.

7. _____

8. _____

9. _____

10. _____

Getting Started: Opinion Paragraphs

Name _____

Supporting Sentences

> An **opinion paragraph** includes an opinion statement, supporting sentences, and a conclusion.
> - The **opinion statement** expresses the writer's feelings about a topic.
> - **Supporting sentences** give reasons supported by facts and examples that answer the question *Why?* about the writer's opinion.
> - Supporting sentences are included in an order that makes sense.

For each opinion below, write three supporting sentences with reasons and vivid facts or examples. Write the sentences in order from most important to least important. Use transitional words or phrases to connect your sentences.

Opinion: How you dress says as much about you as how you treat people does.

_____
_____
_____
_____
_____

Opinion: Movies are much more interesting than TV programs.

_____
_____
_____
_____
_____

Opinion: Biographies are more interesting than novels.

_____
_____
_____
_____
_____

Opinion: People don't know how to behave in movie theaters these days.

_____
_____
_____
_____
_____

SECTION 1 EXPRESSING AND INFLUENCING

WORKBOOK PLUS **Grade 7:** Section 1 Expressing and Influencing *(Use with pupil book pp. 387–391.)*
Skill: Students will write supporting sentences with reasons, facts, and examples.

The Writing Process: Focus Skill

Name _____

Supporting Your Opinion

Opinion: Traveling by train can be interesting, but it has some disadvantages.

Weak Reasons	Strong Reasons
Advantage: Trains have comfortable seats.	**Advantage:** I see so much of the countryside from the window of a train.
Disadvantage: There's not enough stuff to do.	**Disadvantage:** Train trips often take many hours, and I get tired of sitting for all that time.

Make a T-chart for these two points of view. Write two to four reasons to support each point of view.

Opinion: Space exploration has many benefits, but it also has some disadvantages.

Advantages of Space Exploration	Disadvantages of Space Exploration
_____	_____
_____	_____
_____	_____
_____	_____
_____	_____
_____	_____
_____	_____
_____	_____
_____	_____
_____	_____
_____	_____

Grade 7: Unit 9   Opinion   *(Use with pupil book page 405.)*
Skill: Students will list reasons to support an opinion.

UNIT 9 OPINION

WORKBOOK PLUS

The Writing Process: Focus Skill

Name _____

Elaborating Your Reasons

Opinion
Our town needs an animal shelter, but it will be difficult to build one.

Reason
Stray dogs and cats create a health problem for our town.

Detail
1. 30% of stray dogs caught last year had rabies.

Detail
2. Stray animals don't look healthy.

Reason
Finding a place to build an animal shelter will be a problem.

Detail
3. An animal shelter needs lots of space.

Detail
4. Animal shelters are loud, so people don't want them next to their homes.

Identify the most vivid details and those that relate most directly to the reason for the opinion shown. In the spaces below, list the strong and weak details and explain your choices. Then rewrite the weak details to make them stronger.

Strong Details _____
_____
_____
_____

Weak Details _____
_____
_____
_____

158 WORKBOOK PLUS

Grade 7: Unit 9 Opinion *(Use with pupil book pages 406–407.)*
Skill: Students will distinguish between strong and weak supporting details and will rewrite weak details.

The Writing Process: Focus Skill

Name _____

Organizing Your Reasons

Follow these steps to organize your reasons.
- Keep the reasons that provide the best support for your opinion. Delete any weak reasons.
- Find your most important reason, and put that one first or last. If your opinion has two points of view, order the reasons for both points of view.

Read the reasons listed below. Cross out the reason that doesn't support the opinion shown.

Opinion: Growing your own vegetables has advantages and disadvantages.

You can have fresh vegetables at dinner.
You can see in action some of the concepts you learned in science class.
Weeding and watering both take a lot of time.
I don't like doing other chores, such as mowing the lawn.
It's frustrating when plants don't grow well.
Taking care of plants teaches responsibility.

Decide which reasons are advantages and which are disadvantages. Write them in the correct column of the T-chart below. Show them in order from most important to least important. Then answer the questions below the chart.

Advantages	Disadvantages

Which reason did you put first under Advantages? Why do you think this is the most important advantage of having a vegetable garden?

_____
_____
_____

Grade 7: Unit 9   Opinion   (Use with pupil book page 408.)
Skill: Students will distinguish between strong and weak reasons for an opinion and will organize the strong reasons by order of importance.

The Writing Process: Focus Skill

Name _____

Writing with Voice

Opinion: Team sports are more fun than individual sports.

Weak Voice	Strong Voice
In my opinion, team sports are much more fun than individual sports. On a team, you are not alone. You are sharing the experience of working together. It is much more fun.	Ask any athlete what's more fun: playing on a team or doing a sport by yourself. You'll always get the same answer—being part of a team! I love team sports for the laughs in the locker room, on the bus, and on the field.

Write a paragraph that tells your opinion about each statement below. Be sure to engage your readers by letting your own voice come through. Try to use the clearest, most concise language to express your feelings.

1. We learn more from our failures than from our successes.

   _____
   _____
   _____
   _____
   _____
   _____

2. Studying history helps us make better decisions.

   _____
   _____
   _____
   _____
   _____
   _____

Grade 7: Unit 9 Opinion *(Use with pupil book page 409.)*
Skill: Students will write opinions using their own voice.

The Writing Process: Focus Skill

Name _____

Introductions and Conclusions

Opinion: I'm glad our cafeteria has added vegetarian dishes to the menu.

Strong Introduction	
Ask a question.	Hamburgers again? That question hasn't crossed my lips all year. Our cafeteria now has great vegetarian dishes.
Describe a scene.	Walk down to the cafeteria at lunch one day, and watch how many students choose the salad bar. Everyone enjoys having more vegetarian dishes on the menu.
Give an example.	I used to dread buying lunch at school. Now I look forward to it. The food is so much better since they put vegetarian dishes on the menu.

Strong Conclusion
I'm not saying that lunch in the cafeteria is perfect, but it is certainly a lot better. This improvement happened because students and teachers worked together. If we can change the lunch menu for the better, just think how much else we can accomplish.

Read the opinion below. Write three strong introductions, using each of the strategies shown above. Then write a conclusion that leaves your readers thinking.

Opinion: Art class is relaxing and educational.

Introduction: Ask a question.

_____
_____

Introduction: Describe a scene.

_____
_____

Introduction: Give an example.

_____
_____

Conclusion:

_____
_____

The Writing Process

Name _____

Revising an Opinion Essay

Have I   yes
- written an introduction that gets my readers thinking?   ☐
- given the writing my own voice?   ☐
- included details and facts that support my opinion statement?   ☐
- put the details in order from most to least important?   ☐
- written a conclusion that leaves my readers thinking?   ☐

Revise the following opinion essay to make it better. Use the checklist above to help you. Check off each box as you work on your revision. You can use the spaces above the lines, on the sides, and below the paragraph for your changes.

Opinion: The world is a smaller place because of computers.

    I think the world is getting smaller and smaller, and it is all because of computers. Just think about it. Thanks to the Internet, small businesses can now compete for cybersales with major companies in other countries, even on other continents. Each and every day the number of e-mail messages far surpasses the piles of letters handled by the post office. Students can use the libraries of foreign universities to do research. You can buy stocks, books, or anything at all, and look up just about anything and find it, no matter where in the world.

The Writing Process: Revising Strategies

Name _____

Sentence Fluency

Simple sentences	Is reading books a thing of the past? We spend so much time with computers and television! I wonder if this is good or bad.
Complex sentence	Reading books may be a thing of the past now that computers and television consume so much of our free time—and I wonder whether that is a good thing or a bad thing.

Write two introductions for each of the opinions below. First, write an introduction using a few simple sentences. Then write another, using a complex sentence. When you've finished, think about which style reflects your voice and your point of view.

Opinion: The library needs more science fiction books and fewer Shakespeare plays.

Simple Sentences: _____
_____
_____
_____

Complex Sentence: _____
_____
_____
_____

Opinion: Eighteen-year-olds are too young to drive responsibly.

Simple Sentences: _____
_____
_____
_____

Complex Sentence: _____
_____
_____
_____

Grade 7: Unit 9 Opinion *(Use with pupil book page 413.)*
Skill: Students will write simple sentences and combine them into complex sentences.

The Writing Process: Focus Skill

Supporting Your Goal

Goal: persuade the school to replace the water fountains with purified-water dispensers

Weak Reason	Strong Reason
The water from the fountains is cloudy from time to time.	Studies have shown that the water in the fountains is toxic.

Weak Elaboration	Strong Elaboration: Fact
Opinion: Toxic water tastes icky.	A lab found that the water fountains contain dangerous levels of lead.

Strong Elaboration: Example
I had to go to the nurse after drinking from a fountain yesterday.

Write three reasons to persuade your audience to work toward a goal. Elaborate on the reasons by providing a fact and an example for each reason.

Goal	Reasons	Facts and Examples
persuade classmates to donate clothes for the town's homeless families		

Grade 7: Unit 10 Persuasion *(Use with pupil book page 442.)*
Skill: Students will support a goal by providing reasons and then elaborating with facts and examples.

Evaluating Your Reasons

Goal: persuade my parents to let me go on a class trip to a newspaper printing plant

Weak: Doesn't Support Goal	Strong: Supports Goal
I like watching the news on TV.	I'm considering a career as a reporter.

Weak: Inaccurate	Strong: Accurate
I won't be able to get a job as a reporter if I don't go.	The trip may help me decide whether I want to work for a newspaper or in TV.

Weak: May Not Matter to Audience	Strong: Probably Will Matter to Audience
I cleaned my room last week.	The same teachers have chaperoned the trip for the last three years.

Evaluate the reasons given for the goal below. Tell which reasons are strong. List the weak reasons by category. Then rewrite the weak reasons to make them stronger.

Goal: persuade classmates to raise money for school supplies for poor children overseas

Reasons:
1. The class that raises the most money gets a pizza party, served by the principal.
2. These children will never have fulfilling lives.
3. These children can't afford supplies such as pens and paper.
4. Some other schools raise money for various causes.
5. The U.S. government sends aid to these schools.

Strong: _____

Strong: _____

Weak—Doesn't Support Goal: _____

Weak—Inaccurate: _____

Weak—May Not Matter to Audience: _____

The Writing Process: Focus Skill

Name _____

Using Persuasive Strategies

Goal: persuade classmates to volunteer at a soup kitchen

Objection	I'm too busy with homework and friends to volunteer.
Answer	You and your friends can volunteer together for as little as an hour or two each week.
Precedent	Some students in our school volunteer already.
Benefit	The school gives extra credit to students who do volunteer work.

For each goal below, write an objection that the audience may have, and write an answer to that objection. Then cite a precedent for the action. Finally, mention a benefit of working toward the goal.

Goal: persuade my parents to let me have my own computer

1. Objection: _____

   _____

   Answer: _____

   _____

2. Precedent: _____

   _____

3. Benefit: _____

   _____

Goal: persuade our teacher to let us choose some of the books we'll read this year

4. Objection: _____

   _____

   Answer: _____

   _____

5. Precedent: _____

   _____

6. Benefit: _____

WORKBOOK PLUS

Grade 7: Unit 10 Persuasion *(Use with pupil book page 444.)*
Skill: Students will predict objections to goals and will use persuasive strategies to answer those objections.

The Writing Process: Focus Skill

Name _____

Organizing Your Argument

Goal: persuade classmates to help with a fundraiser for the computer lab

Reasons
1. We don't have enough computers for everybody.
2. The school has no money in the budget to upgrade the computer lab.
3. Organizing a fundraiser would be a useful learning experience for the class.

Read the goal. Number the reasons from most important to least important (1 = most important). Then write an argument using the reasons and whatever transitional words you need.

Goal: persuade a friend to work with you to produce a school play

Reason _____: *The Man Who Came to Dinner* is a really funny play.

Reason _____: You'll like all the people in the theater group.

Reason _____: I really need the help.

Reason _____: We'll have a lot of fun together.

Reason _____: The experience will help if you want to join the high school theater group next year.

_____
_____
_____
_____
_____
_____
_____
_____

Grade 7: Unit 10   Persuasion   *(Use with pupil book page 445.)*
Skill: Students will write reasons to support a goal and will organize them by order of importance.

WORKBOOK PLUS 167

The Writing Process: Focus Skill

Name _____

Introductions and Conclusions

Goal: persuade the town to clean up a forest that has become a dumping ground

Introduction: Describe a scene.	Think of a fragrant, peaceful woodland. Now look closer. Do you see the pile of rusty barbed wire among the trees? Now think about getting cut by that same wire.
Introduction: Ask a question.	What's happening to our local forest? Do we want to turn a great natural resource into a garbage dump?
Conclusion: Address your audience.	The town forest is a gift that our ancestors passed on to us. If we all work to keep our forest clean, we can offer a lifetime of learning and pleasure to future generations. Keep the forest green. If we don't, who will?
Conclusion: End with a warning.	The forest is a vital part of a fragile environment that includes the town reservoir. Stop the dumping, or its effects on our town will be catastrophic.

Choose one goal below and write an introduction and a conclusion. To craft a strong introduction, ask a question of your audience, describe a scene, or tell an anecdote. Then conclude by calling your audience to action, by using a figure of speech, or by warning your audience of the consequences of not doing what you propose.

Goal: persuade the principal to offer a karate class as part of the curriculum

Goal: persuade the principal to let students take a short nap in the afternoon

Introduction: _____
_____
_____
_____
_____
_____

Conclusion: _____
_____
_____
_____
_____
_____

Grade 7: Unit 10 Persuasion *(Use with pupil book pages 446–447.)*
Skill: Students will write an introduction and a conclusion for a persuasive essay.

The Writing Process: Focus Skill

Name _____

Writing with Voice

Goal: persuade a local store owner to stock Redbird jeans

Formal Language	Informal Language
According to my research, Redbird is one of the most popular brands in the country, selling more than 25 million pairs of jeans a year.	My classmates and I live in Redbird jeans. They're the best!

Negative Voice	Positive Voice
I've never seen a decent pair of jeans for sale in your store. Don't you know what your customers want?	I've been a loyal customer of your store for several years. It's a great store. In fact, there's only one way I think it could be any better—if you carried Redbird jeans.

Read each goal below. Then, for each audience listed, write a brief argument in favor of the goal. Be sure to use a positive voice, and choose formal or informal language based on the audience.

Goal: persuade each audience to support a youth center in town

Audience: Teenagers _____

_____

_____

Audience: City Council members _____

_____

_____

Goal: persuade each audience to support an exchange-student program

Audience: Students _____

_____

_____

Audience: Principal _____

_____

_____

Grade 7: Unit 10 Persuasion *(Use with pupil book page 448.)*
Skill: Students will choose the appropriate voice for addressing various audiences.

The Writing Process

Revising a Persuasive Essay

Name _____

Have I
- written an introduction that states my goal and hooks my audience?
- given at least three persuasive reasons to support my goal?
- used facts and examples to back up my reasons, in an order that makes sense?
- written in a persuasive, positive, and consistent voice?
- concluded by restating my goal and urging my audience to act?

yes
☐
☐
☐
☐
☐

Revise the following persuasive essay to make it better. Use the checklist above to help you. Check off the boxes as you cover each point. Use the extra space and the margins for your revisions.

Goal: persuade classmates to start an investment club

> If you ask me, I think it would be a great idea for us to form an investment club. Here's why. First of all, a lot of kids do it. A broker downtown told me that she has $50,000 invested for people our age. It would be a great way to learn about the stock market. We could use the Internet to look up stock prices. We might even visit the stockbroker's office and really see the inside stuff for ourselves. The second and more important reason is that we'd learn how to make good investment decisions. The investment club at McKinley has made over $150 so far this year. We could simply follow the performance of several stocks from day to day, or we could raise some money and actually invest it. What do you think?

The Writing Process: Revising Strategies

Name _____

Elaborating: Details

Few details	The equipment in the gym is old and not good for students to use.
Elaborated with details	The rowing machine in our gym is twenty years old. It's missing parts. Dilapidated equipment like that is dangerous for students to use.

Add precise details to elaborate each of the sentences below.

1. We now have only three minutes to get from class to class. It is hard for kids to do everything they have to do.

   _____
   _____
   _____
   _____

2. If our newspaper had pictures, it would be a lot more fun. I know lots of kids who would turn in stuff.

   _____
   _____
   _____
   _____

3. Students could help out in the park. The town could hire them during times when they aren't in school.

   _____
   _____
   _____
   _____

4. Here's what we can do to raise money. We can sell things.

   _____
   _____
   _____
   _____

Grade 7: Unit 10 Persuasion *(Use with pupil book page 451.)*
Skill: Students will elaborate sentences by adding precise details.

Getting Started: Expository Paragraphs

Name _____

Supporting Sentences

Look at the picture and read the captions. Use the picture and captions to help you write supporting sentences for the topic sentence below. Link your sentences with transitional words and phrases.

Photographers take pictures for newspapers and magazines.

Reporters interview people, ask questions, and then tell the story for newspapers and magazines.

Video technicians record events on videotape for TV broadcasts.

News coverage requires the combined effort of a wide variety of people. _____

_____
_____
_____
_____
_____
_____
_____
_____
_____
_____
_____
_____
_____
_____
_____

The Writing Process: Focus Skill

Name _____

Organizing Your Essay

Look at the details for newspaper and book. Write the details in the Venn diagram.

Newspaper	Book
printed on paper	one writer
published daily or weekly	printed on paper
many topics	covers one topic, generally
current information	information may be outdated
factual data	published yearly, at best
many writers	topic researched well
topics researched well	factual data

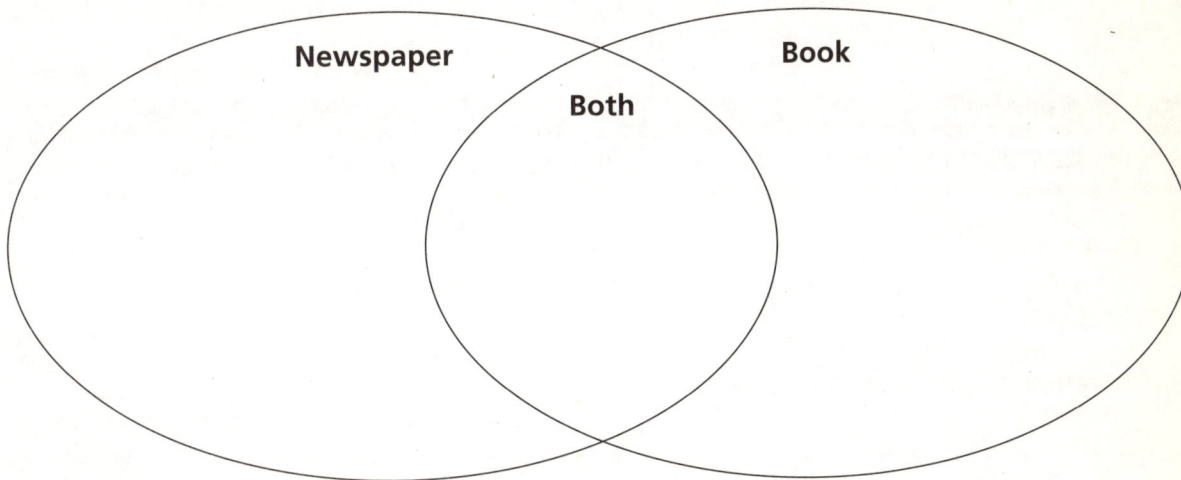

Which form of organization would best present the details of an essay comparing and contrasting books and newspapers?

_____

Create an outline that arranges your details in this way.

_____
_____
_____
_____
_____
_____
_____

Grade 7: Unit 11 Compare-Contrast (Use with pupil book pages 489–490.)
Skill: Students will organize a compare-contrast essay.

UNIT 11 COMPARE-CONTRAST

WORKBOOK PLUS

The Writing Process: Focus Skill

Name _____

Introductions and Conclusions

Strong Introductions	
Question	Do you consider wool just for winter and cotton for summer? Well, guess again!
Anecdote	After enduring seven hours of bothersome itching, I raced home and tore off my new wool sweater. "From now on, it's cotton for me!" I exclaimed.
Surprising fact	While T-shirts and ski caps are fairly modern inventions, the practice of using wool and cotton as textiles can be traced back thousands of years.

Strong Conclusion
For its versatility, comfort, and cost, I'll always choose cotton over wool.

Write three introductions for a compare-contrast essay on the following topic: *Men's fashions versus women's fashions*. Then write a strong conclusion that sums up your major ideas on the topic.

Introduction—Question: _____

_____

_____

Introduction—Anecdote: _____

_____

_____

Introduction—Surprising Fact: _____

_____

_____

Conclusion: _____

_____

_____

Grade 7: Unit 11 Compare-Contrast (Use with pupil book page 491.)
Skill: Students will write introductions and a conclusion for a compare-contrast essay.

The Writing Process: Focus Skill

Name _____

Topic Sentences

Similarities, Then Differences	
Similarities	**Differences**
Karate and boxing are two similar forms of unarmed combat.	Karate and boxing both involve powerful arm movements, but that's where their similarities end.

Feature-by-Feature
When it comes to training, karate and boxing have their own unique methods.

Subject-by-Subject
Karate is a Japanese form of self-defense with a fascinating history.

Think about yourself and someone you know well. Write topic sentences for a compare-contrast essay, using the three styles shown above. Then write a strong conclusion that sums up your ideas.

Similarities, Then Differences:
_____
_____
_____

Feature-by-Feature:
_____
_____
_____

Subject-by-Subject:
_____
_____
_____

Strong Conclusion:
_____
_____
_____

Grade 7: Unit 11 Compare-Contrast *(Use with pupil book page 492.)*
Skill: Students will write topic sentences and a conclusion for a compare-contrast essay.

Revising a Compare-Contrast Essay

Have I
- created an introduction that captures the reader's attention?
- stated my main idea clearly in a topic sentence?
- added details to show similarities and differences?
- written a strong conclusion?

yes
☐
☐
☐
☐

Revise the following essay. Use the checklist above to help you. Check off each box as you revise. You can use the spaces above the line, on the side, and below the paragraph for your changes.

Lizards and Snakes

Scientists have gathered various forms of evidence that snakes and lizards developed from a common ancestor a long time ago, like about 100 million years. Snakes and lizards have a lot of similarities and differences. They are different mostly because most lizards have legs and snakes do not. Both lizards and snakes are reptiles, which means they are cold-blooded so their body temperature is about the same as the temperature of their environment. Lizards eat small animals and insects. Snakes do too, but lizards also eat plants.

The largest snakes grow to about thirty feet. Lizards grow to only about nine or ten feet long. But lizards can move much faster than snakes. The speediest lizards can run as fast as eighteen miles per hour. Snakes can only move as much as seven miles per hour.

The Writing Process: Revising Strategies

Name _____

Elaborating: Word Choice

Repetitive	Leah's story is **funny**, and mine is **funny**, but Tom's is **not funny**.
Elaborated with synonyms and antonyms	Leah's story is **funny**, and mine is **hilarious**, but Tom's is **solemn**.

Write a sentence comparing each subject pair. Use the word in parentheses and a synonym in each sentence.

1. Two athletes' performances **(graceful)**

   _____
   _____

2. Two books or movies **(fascinating)**

   _____
   _____

3. Two skills or school subjects **(effortlessly)**

   _____
   _____

Write a sentence contrasting each subject pair. Use the word provided and an antonym in each sentence.

4. Organization of two pieces of writing **(scattered)**

   _____
   _____

5. Two drivers **(cautiously)**

   _____
   _____

6. Two artists' styles **(realistic)**

   _____
   _____

Grade 7: Unit 11   Compare-Contrast   (Use with pupil book page 495.)
Skill: Students will write compare-contrast sentences, using antonyms and synonyms.

The Writing Process: Focus Skill

Finding the Best Information

> You can find information for a research report by interviewing an expert or by reading facts from books, CD-ROMs, microfilm or microfiche, or the Internet. To evaluate your information, ask yourself the following questions:
> - Is the information related to my topic?
> - Does the source provide facts rather than opinions?
> - Is this source reliable? Does it offer information from a professional or an expert in the field?
> - Is the information up-to-date?

Look at the description of each report given below. List at least two reliable sources that you could consult for information. Be sure your source description contains specific details related to your topic.

1. Who planned and completed the Erie Canal in New York in the early 1800s? How did its completion affect towns and cities along its route?

2. If businesses use recycled glass, metals, or paper instead of new natural resources, is it more expensive, or can they save money?

3. How have weather patterns in Western Europe changed in the last 100 years?

4. Who are the most successful athletes since 1968 in Olympic track and field events such as running?

5. In all the world, which nation has the largest population?

The Writing Process: Focus Skill

Name _____

Organizing Your Report

> I. Comics—popular form of visual storytelling
>   A. Types of comics
>   1. Comic strips: short series of related cartoons
>   2. Comic books: magazine format with longer stories
>   3. Both can be humorous or tell adventurous stories.
>   B. History of comics
>   1. Earliest comic strips—just before 1900
>   2. Full-length comic books—popular in 1930s

With the information below, create an outline for a research report on the sport of dragon-boat racing. Use the outline above as a model. Draw a line through facts that are repetitive or unimportant.

- Average length of race: 250 meters to 1,000 meters
- Dragon-boat racing began in China.
- Another sport with worldwide popularity is soccer.
- Average time of race: three to six minutes
- Traditionally, races held as part of yearly festival
- According to legends, started 400 B.C.
- Gymnastics and skiing other sports with long history
- Dragon-boat crew: twenty-two members, including twenty who paddle
- Boats colorful, shaped to look like dragons with fierce heads
- Has spread through Asia and to United States and Canada

_____
_____
_____
_____
_____
_____
_____
_____
_____
_____
_____
_____
_____

Grade 7: Unit 12   Research Report   *(Use with pupil book pages 523–524.)*
Skill: Students will create an outline for a research report.

The Writing Process: Focus Skill

Name _____

Writing from an Outline

Section of an Outline	Writing from the Outline
I. Many kings, queens, emperors began reigns as children A. Pu Yi, China's last emperor, 1908—two years old	Children have sat on the thrones of many countries throughout history. In 1908, China crowned as its last emperor a two-year-old boy named Pu Yi.

Write a paragraph from the outline section given below. Be sure to start with a strong, clear topic sentence that gives the main idea. Then support the idea with sentences about subtopics and details.

Frederick Douglass

I. Born a slave; became most powerful African American leader of nineteenth century
   A. Major achievements that he helped bring about
      1. During his life
         a. Most important: 1865, Thirteenth Amendment to Constitution—banned slavery
         b. 1868: Fourteenth Amendment—citizenship to former slaves
         c. 1870: Fifteenth Amendment—all adult males (including African Americans) right to vote
      2. After his death (1895)
         a. 1920: Nineteenth Amendment—women the right to vote

_____
_____
_____
_____
_____
_____
_____
_____
_____
_____

The Writing Process: Focus Skill

Name _____

Introductions and Conclusions

Weak Introduction
Advertising companies help sell things. The word *advertising* comes from French and means "to call attention to." That is what advertisers do.

Strong Introduction
What is the source of advertisers' power over consumers? Is it catchy jingles we hum unconsciously or visual images we can't forget?

Weak Conclusion
We consumers should take advertisements with a grain of salt. After all, how else would we know we needed mouthwash or fabric softener?

Strong Conclusion
Advertisements help us make better buying decisions. However, as advertising attempts to influence those decisions, we often feel bombarded and manipulated.

Write an introduction and conclusion for the following paragraph.

From Lake Itasca in northwestern Minnesota, the Mississippi River flows almost 2,350 miles before spilling into the Gulf of Mexico. The river is undoubtedly our major inland waterway. The Mississippi and its tributaries irrigate an area of approximately 1.25 million square miles, watering the nation's chief agricultural areas. It is estimated that some 60 percent of this country's inland waterway freight is transported on the Mississippi. That freight includes agricultural products (such as corn and wheat), steel, coal, and petrochemical products.

Introduction: _____
_____
_____
_____
_____

Conclusion: _____
_____
_____
_____
_____
_____
_____

Grade 7: Unit 12 Research Report (Use with pupil book page 529.)
Skill: Students will write a strong introduction and conclusion for a research report.

Revising a Research Report

Have I
- written a strong introduction that presents the main topic?
- organized the report in a logical manner?
- given my readers the facts as well as colorful details?
- included an interesting conclusion that sums up my main point?

yes
☐
☐
☐
☐

Revise the following research report to make it better. Use the checklist above to help you. Check off each box as you revise. Use the fact list to help you. You can use the spaces above the lines, on the sides, and below the paragraph for your changes.

- First played in France during twelfth or thirteenth century
- 1874: Major Wingfield introduced equipment and rules for playing on grass courts.
- 1877: First tournament played on grass courts at Wimbledon, England
- Today: Tournaments are played worldwide, in countries such as Australia, France, Argentina, England, the United States, Sweden, and Zimbabwe, to name just a few.

Tennis Comes of Age

The game of tennis goes back a long time. An early form of the game was first played in France. True modern tennis, however, was begun by Major Walter C. Wingfield in 1873. A year later, Major Wingfield introduced equipment and rules.

Today, tennis players come from all over the world.

The first tennis tournament was played in Wimbledon, England.

The first U.S. Men's Championship was played in 1881 in Newport, Rhode Island. Tennis is played everywhere.

The Writing Process: Revising Strategies

Name _____

Elaborating: High-Interest Details

Few details	A turning point in the history of fashion took place in the 1300s. Clothing became much fancier. The European nobility stepped out in fine clothes.
With high-interest details	A turning point in the history of fashion took place in the 1300s. Clothing became much fancier. Fashionable members of the nobility wore close-fitting waistcoats cinched by elaborately jeweled belts. Decorative edging called *dagging* trimmed many garments, and coats sported dozens of buttons.

Improve the following research report by adding high-interest details. Use the bulleted facts to capture your audience. You may wish to write the report in more than one paragraph.

Abraham Lincoln's early life is as interesting as his presidency. He lived on the frontier, so it was hard to get an education. Lincoln did many different kinds of jobs before turning to politics and the law. Few Presidents have had the varied experiences Lincoln had.
- He had less than a year of formal schooling.
- One of his jobs was helping guide a flatboat down the Mississippi River.
- In his youth, he often walked many miles to borrow a book.
- Other jobs held by Lincoln were postmaster, storekeeper, and surveyor.
- Books were rare on the frontier in Lincoln's youth.

_____
_____
_____
_____
_____
_____
_____
_____
_____

Grade 7: Unit 12 Research Report (Use with pupil book page 532.)
Skill: Students will elaborate their reports with high-interest details.

Supporting Sentences

Lead sentence	When I picked up that harmonica, I decided I wouldn't stop practicing until I could play a tune.
Supporting details	My plan was to spend an hour playing the harmonica every day when I got home from school even though at first it sounded like a broken radiator.

Read about the following topic and look at the picture. Then supply a lead sentence, at least three supporting sentences, and a concluding sentence.

Topic: A group of seventh graders hikes to the top of a mountain to watch the sun rise.

Lead Sentence: _____

_____

_____

Supporting Sentences: _____

_____

_____

_____

_____

_____

Concluding Sentence: _____

_____

_____

The Writing Process: Focus Skill

Name _____

Organizing Your Narrative

- Reread your freewriting.
- Order the events by numbering them.
- Make a chart to order your events. Add details that describe each event.
- Make sure that each event stays on the topic.

This student explored an idea for a personal narrative by freewriting. Now it's time to organize these details. Cross out sentences that don't stick to the main topic. Sequence the remaining events from 1 to 5. Then organize the main events in the chart below. Add details to elaborate each event.

    We loaded the car for our trip—suitcases, pillows, snacks, bikes. What a mess! Me, Mom, and Dad. Oh! Our neighbor's cute new puppy is outside playing. Finally, cruising along the highway, no problem. What's that? Smoke! Thick, black, smelly stuff, pouring from the hood. It was awfully nice of that stranger to stop. He had tools. His car was cool—antique convertible, bright red. We were stranded for hours before help arrived. Hot! Boring! I found my missing marble wedged under the seat. The man and my Dad fixed the radiator. Got the old car running again!

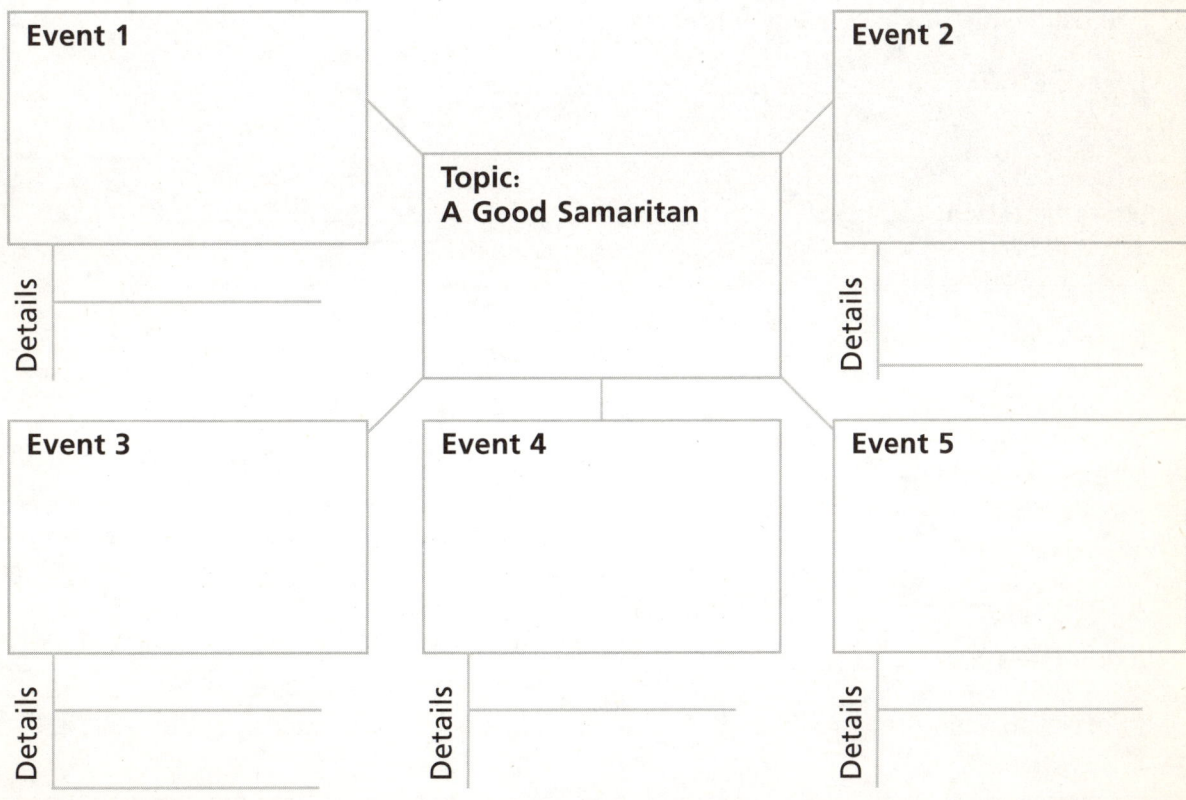

UNIT 13   PERSONAL NARRATIVE

Grade 7: Unit 13   Personal Narrative   (Use with pupil book page 570.)
Skill: Students will organize details from a freewrite, using a chart.

WORKBOOK PLUS   185

The Writing Process: Focus Skill

Name _____

Good Beginnings

Weak Beginning	Strong Beginnings		
	Describe an action	Ask a question	Express an emotion
I like to play the trumpet.	My trumpet swayed to the rhythm of our music, counting out the 4/4 time.	Have you ever heard Miles Davis blow out a note that makes the birds stop to listen?	It was almost time for my solo. The look in my mother's eyes told me I could do it.

Draft three strong beginnings to replace each of the following weak beginnings.

1. The pilot's announcement scared me.

   Describe an Action: _____
   _____

   Ask a Question: _____
   _____

   Express an Emotion: _____
   _____

2. I hoped the pie would be ready for the party tonight.

   Describe an Action: _____
   _____

   Ask a Question: _____
   _____

   Express an Emotion: _____
   _____

3. I was late to school.

   Describe an Action: _____
   _____

   Ask a Question: _____

   Express an Emotion: _____
   _____

WORKBOOK PLUS

Grade 7: Unit 13 Personal Narrative *(Use with pupil book page 571.)*
Skill: Students will write strong beginnings for personal narratives, using three different strategies.

The Writing Process: Focus Skill

Name _____

Writing with Voice

Weak Voice	Strong Voice
We went to the beach. My friend Rose and I made a sand castle. Later we played in the water.	It was a day I guess I'll never forget, warm and sunny. The beach, the ocean, and the sky seemed to stretch endlessly before us, and time seemed to stop. The sand castle we were building became grander and bigger. Suddenly a wave washed over the sand castle Rose and I had spent the morning carefully creating.

The narrative paragraphs below sound wooden and dull. Revise them by choosing words that carry your voice. Carefully construct and punctuate your sentences to show emotion.

1. My boots slipped on the icy steps. I hoped I would make it up the steps with Grandmother's groceries. I began to wonder if I really would.

   _____
   _____
   _____
   _____
   _____
   _____
   _____

2. I was excited to see my very first paycheck. It seemed like a lot of money. I wondered if it was a mistake. Then I realized that it was incorrect. Now what should I do?

   _____
   _____
   _____
   _____
   _____
   _____
   _____

Grade 7: Unit 13 Personal Narrative *(Use with pupil book page 572.)*
Skill: Students will rewrite personal narratives, using a strong voice.

The Writing Process: Focus Skill

Name _____

Good Endings

Weak Ending	Strong Ending
I wish I could say it was the end of a perfect vacation, but I can't.	With the sound of each crashing wave against the rocks outside our window, we felt more sure that we wanted out of there, and fast. It will be a long time before I cavalierly agree to stay the weekend in a "haunted" house.

Draft two endings for the following paragraph. Conclude by telling what the character learned or by repeating a phrase or idea mentioned before. Place a check mark next to the version you like better.

    Have you ever heard the saying, "If you don't like the weather, wait a minute"? I was waiting for my brother and sister, due home from the matinee in town. It had been sunny and warm when they left. At 6:00 P.M. the meterologist on Channel 4 predicted high winds and thunderstorms. I looked up and saw a bolt of lightning flash against the dark sky. Suddenly, the lights went out. Then I heard a big bang from the kitchen.

Ending That Tells What You Have Learned: _____

_____

_____

_____

_____

_____

_____

Ending That Repeats a Phrase or Idea: _____

_____

_____

_____

_____

_____

_____

_____

Grade 7: Unit 13 Personal Narrative *(Use with pupil book page 573.)*
Skill: Students will draft two conclusions for a narrative, then choose the stronger ending.

The Writing Process

Revising a Personal Narrative

Have I
- grabbed my reader's interest with a strong introduction?
- presented all events in the order in which they happened?
- included only details that are important to the story?
- used a tone and language that allow my voice to come through?
- provided a conclusion that doesn't leave my reader hanging?

yes
☐
☐
☐
☐
☐

Use the editing checklist to help you revise the paragraph from a personal narrative. Use the space above the lines and in the margins to write your revisions.

    This morning, I was thinking it would be a great trip. I finished packing my last bag. I looked out the window and saw the neighbor bring out the trash. Everyone else in my family seemed sad. When I stepped onto the train I understood their sadness. I had to say good-bye to each member of my family. I finally found my seat. I looked out the window and said good-bye to everything I knew.

The Writing Process: Revising Strategies

Name _____

Elaborating: Word Choice

Without figurative language	The delicate porcelain clown had sad, expressive eyes.
With a simile	The delicate porcelain clown had eyes as sad as rain clouds.
With a metaphor	The porcelain clown's eyes were dark storm clouds ready to burst with rain.

Use comparisons to make these narrative paragraphs more interesting. Revise the narratives, adding at least one simile and one metaphor to each.

1. I begged and pleaded and threatened to leave home, but it didn't do any good. My mother thought the after-school film class would interfere with my homework. Finally, we made a bargain. If I got straight A's for one quarter, the next quarter I could take the class. I felt good when my mother finally agreed.

   _____
   _____
   _____
   _____
   _____
   _____

2. When I started taking the sign language course I didn't think I would ever be any good at it. I didn't know any signs, and our teacher taught only in American Sign Language from the very first day. I was scared to try, but my teacher encouraged me, and guess what? By the end of the class I felt confident.

   _____
   _____
   _____
   _____
   _____
   _____

Grade 7: Unit 13 Personal Narrative (Use with pupil book page 576.)
Skill: Students will revise a personal narrative, elaborating with figurative language.

The Writing Process: Focus Skill

Name _____

Developing Plot

The conflict of a story focuses on one person's problem with another person, with nature, or with himself or herself. You can create a plot by setting up a conflict for your characters. Then add obstacles as they deal with the conflict, bringing the action to a high point (climax). In the resolution, tell how the characters solve the problem.

Weak Plot
Nina's dog, Rexie, runs away. She's sad. Rexie finds his way back home later that day.

Strong Plot
Rexie runs away. Nina puts up posters. A caller says she's found Rexie. It's the wrong dog. Nina organizes search teams. They scour the woods and find the injured dog.

Choose one character and one setting from the chart below. Then come up with a possible story plot using this pair. Be creative! List as many details as you can about the conflict, the climax, and the resolution inside the story map.

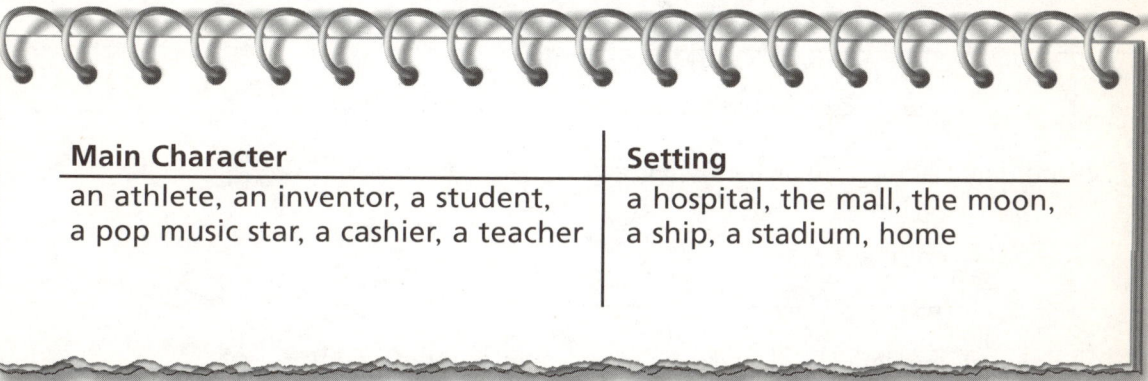

Main Character	Setting
an athlete, an inventor, a student, a pop music star, a cashier, a teacher	a hospital, the mall, the moon, a ship, a stadium, home

Conflict

Climax

Resolution

UNIT 14 STORY

Grade 7: Unit 14 Story (Use with pupil book pages 595–596.)
Skill: Students will develop a strong plot, including conflict, complications, climax, and resolution.

WORKBOOK PLUS

The Writing Process: Focus Skill

Name _____

Dialogue

Without Dialogue	With Dialogue
Sue's room was untidy. Her mother disliked a mess. She reminded Sue to clean it.	"I have asked you twice to do something about this mess," grumbled Sue's mother. Sue gazed absently around her room. "Clean it up today!" ordered her mom.

Rewrite the sentences below, adding dialogue. Choose words that show what each character is like and how he or she is feeling.

1. Claire asked her father if he liked her new haircut. Her father expressed concern.
   _____
   _____

2. The judge announced that I had won the contest. My family shouted from the stands.
   _____
   _____

3. The librarian asked the students to be quiet.
   _____
   _____

4. My little sister apologized for wearing my sweater without asking.
   _____
   _____

5. The coach told the players to try their best.
   _____
   _____

6. Dan stated that sledding is an exciting winter activity. Carlos agreed.
   _____
   _____

The Writing Process: Focus Skill

Name _____

Narrating Your Story

First-person	I saw that it was already dark outside, so I hung the wet clothes quickly.
Limited third-person	Mary peered nervously into the dark back yard. Quickly she hung out the wet things.
Omniscient third-person	Hanging the clothes on the line always made Mary feel as if she were grown-up and on her own. Her mother was proud of her.
Mood: peaceful	As Mary hung the wet clothes at dusk, the lamps from the house cast a warm homey light across the lawn.

Draft two possible story beginnings for each of the situations described below. Experiment with two different points of view and two different moods. Choose the version you like best and place a check mark next to it.

1. A thirteen-year-old boy and his seventy-five-year-old grandmother share the same birthday. They both want to get each other very special birthday gifts, and neither one has very much money.

   Write a beginning for a dramatic story in the first-person point of view.
   _____
   _____

   Write a beginning for a sad story in the limited third-person point of view.
   _____
   _____

2. A rumor gets started about a pond monster in a small lake at the end of a local road. At first, no one takes it seriously, but the more the story gets tossed around, the more people become afraid.

   Write a beginning for a scary story in the first-person point of view.
   _____
   _____

   Write a beginning for a funny story in the omniscient third-person point of view.
   _____
   _____

Grade 7: Unit 14 Story *(Use with pupil book pages 598–599.)*
Skill: Students will write story openings using different points of view and different moods.

The Writing Process

Revising a Story

Have I
- introduced the setting at the beginning of the story?
- created an interesting conflict and stated it clearly?
- chosen one point of view and stuck with it?
- included only events that are important to the main plot?
- told events in an order that makes sense?
- added dialogue to make characters seem real?

yes
☐
☐
☐
☐
☐
☐

Use the checklist to help you revise the following story. Mark your changes in the spaces above the lines, on the sides, and below the paragraph. Check off each box as you revise.

Paula's grandmother worked as a nurse's aide. Her ward needed volunteers. Nanny thought Paula would make a fine volunteer, but Paula disagreed.

Paula didn't want to hurt Nanny's feelings, so she agreed to go. Nanny suggested that Paula visit her pediatric ward. That night, Paula had friends over.

The next day, Nanny took Paula on a tour and introduced her to everyone. The cafeteria was packed! Then she gave me a book and left me with a patient, a young boy. My heart was pounding as I read him the story. When Paula finished reading, the entire ward applauded. They had all been listening!

Paula felt proud. She marched off to ask Nanny where to sign up for the job.

The Writing Process: Revising Strategies

Name _____

Sentence Fluency

Stringy sentences	Every day, the boy would practice in his back yard and as he did, he knew he had to be careful not to start too early and he never did because the sound of the basketball could really get on a person's nerves.
Smooth sentences	Every day, the boy would practice in his back yard. He knew he had to be careful not to start too early, and he never did. The sound of the basketball could really get on a person's nerves.

The following opening paragraph of a story is difficult to read because it has too many long, stringy sentences. Smooth them out by breaking the sentences into shorter sentences of varying length thoughts.

    As they went through the marching maneuvers for the third time, Lisa felt once again how wonderful it was to be part of the school band and practicing right now. This night was different from the many other practice sessions, and it made sense that it was, since the music director, Mr. Burke, had big plans for the band in the coming months. He had spent many extra hours with the band on the practice field, and its sound was improving every day, and that made Lisa stop and think about what a nice man Mr. Burke was and even though he was strict, he really cared about the kids in the band.

_____
_____
_____
_____
_____
_____
_____
_____
_____
_____
_____
_____

Grade 7: Unit 14 Story *(Use with pupil book page 602.)*
Skill: Students will revise a story to smooth out stringy sentences.